Let's Hear It For Herbs!

DOT R. GRIFFIN

*Drawings by Wayne Powell
and the Author*

*Original Designs and Patterns
by the Author*

Iron Mountain Press
Emory, Virginia

ISBN 0-931182-01-8

This Special Edition published and distributed by
IRON MOUNTAIN PRESS
Box 28
Emory, VA 24327

This book is dedicated with much love to my parents who taught me to appreciate the world of plants; and my husband, Ray; and children, Terry, Brad and Carol for their patience, help and encouragement in letting ''Granny'' do her thing.

Table Of Contents

Acknowledgements

I wish to express appreciation to my family and close friends for their assistance in helping with the preparation of this book. Special thanks go to my husband who sacrificed part of his vegetable garden to make room for my herbs and who judged my culinary experiments; To my son, Dr. Terry Griffin, Professor of German at Emory and Henry College and his wife, Nancy, who edited my material; To the staff at Appalachian Information, Inc. in Abingdon, Virginia for use of facilities and for setting the copy; to Kathy Butler who did the design and layout; to Wayne Powell of Perryville, Maryland, for sketching the backgrounds of the chapter headings; To Steven Reynolds of Sisterville, West Virginia, who did the cover photograph of "Granny:" To writer, Helen M. White of Lowell, O., for introducing me to the world of journalism and to the Parkersburg News and the St. Marys Oracle for giving me the opportunity to write, and many, many thanks to the rest of my family—Dr. and Mrs. Brad Griffin of Worcester, Mass., and Mr. and Mrs. Terry Johnson of Gallipolis, O., who shared my enthusiasm in writing about my fun with herbs and kept telling me: "You can do it!".

Dot R. Griffin

St. Marys, W. VA
June, 1978

A Magic Garden

Come with me to a magic garden—one filled with the most enchanting little blossoms and delightful fragrances and where each plant has tricks all its own—an old-fashioned herb garden.

Anyone can have such a garden, whether it be mini-sized or encompassing the "east forty." A strawberry jar will hold as many as nine plants; a sunny window sill, hanging baskets, bare spots in the vegetable and flower beds are all herb-tuckable and the reward will be ten-fold.

Not only do herbs have fragrance, they also have attractive foliage which makes contrasting accents and backgrounds in the flower garden.

Foliage shades of green range from the chartreuse of My Lady's Mantle to the waxy green of germander and frosty blue-green of rue. The grey tones which abound in herbs are perfect foils for pink and yellow flowers. Many artemisias have varied shades of grey; wormwood with its silvery-backed leaves, ghostly-white dusty miller and the grey-green of pontica. Horehound, santolina and lavender contribute still other shades of grey.

Actually, I think herbs are a flower-arranger's dream, for in the herb garden one can find any shape or form one desires. To add lightness to a bouquet one may use feathery fennel, dill or southernwood. Scented geranium's will provide both texture and shape, Erect lemon-scented Prince Ruppert establishes strong lines in vertical arrangements. Oak-leaved geraniums such as Village Hill Hybrid are sharp-toothed and have dark purple markings. Other forms include the skeleton leafs and French lace which has green and white variegated leaves. My favorite geranium for arranging is the Peppermint *P. Tomentosum* which has a deep green velvety "grape leaf."

Lamb's Ear [*Stachys olympica*] has "furry-looking leaves" and it is a delightful herb to grow for children—little animals can be fashioned with it. We grown-ups like to use it in wreaths, flower arrangements and pressed in pressed flower pictures. It is one of the easily grown and propogated herbs which does well in ordinary soil. It also makes a very attractive border.

Another herb with a furry texture is mullein. It is commonly called the "velvet plant," and since it grows quite tall, it is not usually cultivated in the herb garden. It may be found growing along a country roadside and can be harvested from early summer to fall. The stalks are used in vertical arrangements and the rosettes formed at the base of the stalk are sometimes dried and used as focal points in arrangements. Mullein is one of the early day simples. The dried and powdered leaves were boiled with milk and honey to make a remedy for coughs. The dried leaves were also smoked to ease coughing and bronchitis.

Round forms may be found in umbels of dill, coriander, anise, lovage and the seed heads of bergamot. Sweet Cicely, anise and parsley make lacy accents and, of course, the mints are cool and refreshing and sweet basil is shiny and spicy.

Being surrounded with these fascinating plants becomes a challange to use them in every way possible. During our 30 years of growing and experimenting with herbs we have found numerous ways to enjoy herbs, and these we are sharing in the following chapters.

One chapter is devoted to the importance of harvesting and drying the plants at the proper time. Culinary use takes priority at our house for there is no disputing the old adage, "The way to a man's heart is through his stomach." Herbs definitely add zest and imagination to one's cooking. We have included herb butters, salts, seasonings, vinegars, jellies, syrups, flavorings, teas, pickles, relishes, soup bags, appetizers, breads, salads, sandwiches, and recipes for using herbs in cheese, eggs, poultry, fish and meat dishes. We have not neglected desserts either. You will find recipes for cakes, pies, cookies and even ice cream which use herbs as a complementing flavor.

Herbs are a boon to the weight watcher for they cut down on the use of salt and sugar. Herbal teas are beneficial too. Most have both nutritional and healing qualities and they do not introduce poisonous chemicals into the body such as caffeine or tannic acids.

Although we do not list the medicinal uses for herbs except simple remedies such as peppermint teas for the upset stomach; camomile tea to induce slumber; comfrey as a poultice and source of vitamin B-12; sage tea for headaches; and aloe vera, a succulent plant with mucilaginous juice that seems to relieve kitchen burns instantly, we know that modern medicine is returning more and more to the healing herb.

We give recipes for capturing and using the fragrance of herbs in potpourri, sachets, sweet bags, bath salts, bath powders, soaps, hair rinses and deodorizers.

Since it has been proven that herbs are helpful in companion planting, we have included a list of herbs and their contribution to the gardener—what insect or disease it repels and how it benefits certain plants.

It seems that falling asleep has been a problem down through the ages and herbs were much used to induce slumber, so you will find recipes for slumber pillows and patterns for very special dolls to replace the ''nite-nites'' taken to bed by youngsters to comfort and lull them to sleep.

Nor have we forgotten the usefulness of herbs in making one's pet more comfortable. Patterns are included for making catnip and pennyroyal mice, and flea repellent pillows.

One chapter lists the most commonly grown and used herbs, their growing habits and suggestions for their use.

Herbs are also attractive in decorating. Dried and pressed they retain their color in pressed flower pictures. For a change at Christmas why not include some herbal decorations? There are several herbs such as rosemary, thyme and mint which are associated with the birth of Christ and their religious symbolism is traditional in many foreign countries. Patterns for some of these decorations have been included.

Although roses are not considered herbs, it is difficult to imagine an herb garden without them. Our final chapter reviews some of the uses for roses grandmother practiced in her day. Perhaps you too will enjoy making rose beads and preparing rose water.

This magic garden can open up a new world for you. Before long you will be reading everything from that heavy tome *The Herbal of General History of Plants* (1633) by John Gerard, our favorite reference, to short squibs about herbs in the newspapers.

Learning about the lore, myths, superstitions and importance herbs have played in war and peace down through the centuries can add to one's appreciation of the herb garden, and perhaps you will agree with me to the truth of the old saying:

"To grow herbs is to soothe the soul and invite good fortune."

Growing The Plants

Do we have your attention? Fine. Let's begin with some of the easiest and most popular herbs (annuals, biennials and perennials).

Parsley, a biennel, seems to take forever to germinate so it helps to soak the seeds overnight in warm water. The same treatment speeds up nasturtiums.

Chives, shallots and garlic are alliums. Chives may be started from seed and will produce enough plants the first year to supply half the neighborhood. Shallots and garlic bulbs multiply and can be kept producing by planting some of the harvest each year.

Other herbs once established and which will continue to grow every year include: rhubarb, horseradish, comfrey, tansy, sage, valerian, santolina, lavender, lamb's ears, costmary, yarrow, germander, the thymes, mallows, woad, my lady's mantle, lovage, lily-of-the-valley, wintery savory, bergamot, the mints, and the artemisias such as wormwood, pontica, tarragon and southernwood

Sweet woodruff (used in the German Maibowle or May wine) will keep spreading every year if planted in shady spots. It is one herb that will thrive under trees. Burnet, horehound, coral bells, fall crocus (saffron), and camomile are other easily grown perennials.

Annuals include the basils, dill (which will reseed if the bed is not disturbed), summer savory, fennel, catnip, marjoram, pot marigold, water cress, borage and chervil.

One may add to the herb supply with a few trips to the fields and woods. We advise getting a browser's permit from the owner for gathering violets, wild ginger, boneset, snake root, golden seal Mayapple, ginseng, coltsfoot and chicory.

Herbs are not too particular about the soil they grow in—some have more fragrance if the soil is a bit deprived. You plant the seeds and "abacadabra" (well almost) your herb garden will materialize. Culture information is provided on the seed packages, but we find the following instructions work for us. Most of the seeds are tiny so we mix them with a little sand and place on finely worked soil, pressing them down with a flat board. If planted directly in the garden, sprinkle the row with some sifted black peat moss. This gives a pattern for gentle watering so the soil does not form a hard crust and prevent the seedlings from coming through. They will need to be hand-weeded for several weeks and thinned. This is the hardest part—to throw away those extra plants, but be firm. Plants must have room to develop without competition.

If you start the seeds indoors in pots, use sterile soil. Press the seeds in the soil and sift a thin coating of milled sphagnum moss over them to prevent damping off. Set pot in warm water until the top of the soil feels moist. Water from the bottom whenever the top soil becomes dry. When the plants develop the first true leaves, carefully lift the plant up by the leaves with your fingers and transplant to a larger container. Be sure the plants are growing good before transplanting to the garden.

If you do not have time or space to fuss with planting the seeds, you can buy the plants from a reputable nursery (several excellent sources are listed in the back of the book). Three plants of each herb will give a plentiful supply for a family of four.

I keep the perennials and annuals separated, the annuals being easier to cultivate when planted in the vegetable garden. To encourage my husband to give my herbs more space in his garden, I remind him that the herbs are natural repellents and will keep garden pests away from his tomatoes, cabbages, etc.

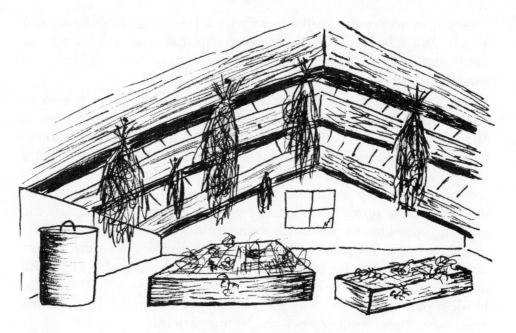

Drying Herbs

Most herbs grow quickly and thrive when pinched back. One can begin snipping off the tender leaves from perennials in May and from annuals in June.

Herbs like thyme, hyssop and mints contain the highest content of volatile oils just before the blossoms open. Cut perennials about one third way down the main stalk and cut off the tender side branches. One can usually get two good harvests a year from the perennials. Cut the herbs which are annuals to the ground.

Gather herbs in the morning after the dew has evaporated. Rinse quickly in cool water. Discard wilted and damaged leaves. Shake off the excess water and tie in very small bunches and hang in the shade (like under a tree) until the water has evaporated. Then take the herbs indoors and hang in an airy space. I hang my herbs on a clothesline stretched across the attic and find that they will usually dry in five days.

When I am certain ALL the moisture has evaporated, I put the herbs into a large paper shopping bag and clip shut. Later I will check again to make sure the plant is perfectly dry and then strip off the leaves and put them into opaque glass jars and seal. I leave the leaves whole until I am ready to make up special seasonings.

Camomile flowers and lavender flowers are cut off at the stem and spread to dry on screens. Large-leaved plants such as comfrey, costmary and scented geraniums which have fleshy stalks, I strip from the stalk and dry on screens. I check them about every two days, turning them over so they will dry quickly. The quicker the leaves dry, the more flavor and fragrance they will retain.

Thyme is a creeper and gets muddy, so it needs at least five cool rinses. I then put it into a French salad basket and give it several swings to shake off the moisture. The basket of thyme is hung in the attic and will dry in several days.

Basil has a tendency to darken unless dried quickly. If possible, pick the basil after a rain shower and the plants have had a chance to dry naturally. Strip the leaves from the stalk and spread them in a single layer on a cookie sheet. Put into the oven set on its lowest temperature and leave ten minutes. By this time the leaves will be practically dry. Complete the drying process by transferring the leaves to an elevated screen in an airy place. Parsley will retain its deep green and special flavor also when dried by this method.

Herbs grown for seed harvest such as coriander, caraway, anise, dill, fennel, sesame and cumin, must be completely ripe when harvested. Test by tapping the plant. If the seeds fall easily, the plant is ready.

I carry a big paper bag into the garden and hold it under the seed heads as I snip them into the bag. To separate the seed and chaff, I put the plants into a pillow case, hang it on the clothesline and flail with an old-fashioned carpet beater.

Another method of separating the chaff from the seed is to place the herb between two sheets laid on a screen and tap with a stick. Sift through screen. Most of the chaff will fall through, the rest can be removed by carefully pouring the seed from one container to another. Performing this chore on a windy day is helpful. Leave the seeds in paper bags until all signs of moisture are gone, then place in opaque jars, seal and label.

Pot marigold petals or raylets pulled from the flower head and spread on newspapers in a warm airy place will dry quickly. Do not wash the blossoms. The rays are a substitute for saffron.

Roses, though not an herb, add bulk and fragrance in sachets, sweet bags and potpourri. Follow the method for screen drying leaves, or if you lack the space, place the petals on newspapers and push them under a bed. The petals MUST be chip dry before storing in paper bags.

Tiny rosebuds from floribundas and ramblers may be dried separately in silica gel, sand or a mixture of corn meal and borax. They make attractive additions to the potpourri jar.

Butterin' Up

Butter can be the "go-between" the zesty herb and vegetables, meat, poultry, egg dishes, sauces and bread. Herb butter is one of the best introductions to herb cookery. The novice gains confidence in experimenting with the butters, which, used with discretion can bring out a robust or a subtle flavor of the herb.

Basic proportion is ¼ cup (half stick oleo) or 2 ounces butter (unsalted butter if available is best), to 1 generous tablespoon of the chopped or minced herb. Melt half of the butter, add the fresh herb and let set for 10 minutes. Then add this to the rest of the softened butter. If dried herbs are used, decrease the proportion to ½ teaspoonsul of the herb, since the dried herb is more potent. Improve the flavor by allowing the dried herb to presoak a few minutes in a little lemon or orange juice.

Herb butters will keep for several days when stored in well-covered jars or crocks in the refrigerator.

If one is serving guests and uncertain about their liking herb-flavored vegetables, leave the vegetables plain and serve the herb butter separately in little salt cellars.

And now for some winning combinations:

Add chopped parsley and/or chives to the butter—enhances new boiled potatoes, baked fish fillets, poached eggs. Parsley combined with a proportion of ¼ goes well with any herb.

Minced tarragon mixed with butter and spread generously inside and outside a roasting chicken is something special. Tarragon butter added to heated liquid from a can of salmon and ¼ cup of vinegar makes a complementary sauce for cold salmon. Tarragon butter may also be used in deviled eggs, adding the butter to the mashed yolk along with a dash of vinegar, mayonnaise, a pinch of salt and a pinch of sugar.

You will agree with Old World cooks who refer to savory as the "bean herb" once you use it in herb butter as a dressing for green beans.

Rosemary butter with a touch of garlic salt has an affinity with lamb chops, corn, cauliflower and broccoli.

Basil butter is good with stewed or creamed tomatoes.

Marjoram butter is great with mushrooms.

Thyme, like parsley, is versatile, blending well with other herbs or used singly on vegetables, especially peas, boiled onions, beets, steamed carrots, eggplant, zucchini and in stuffings.

Dill weed butter is good on boiled potatoes and, like chive butter, adds taste to baked potatoes. Dill seed, ½ teaspoon, ½ teaspoon lemon juice and 2 tablespoons butter, make a sauce for lamb or pork chops.

For a quick herb bread to serve with pasta dishes, slice a loaf of French, Vienna or homemade bread almost through the bottom crust, then spread with herb butter. A dash of garlic salt may be added to the herb butter. Wrap in foil and heat thoroughly in oven.

To make herb sticks, cut 6 weiner buns in half lengthwise, then cut each bun into 4 fingers. Brush cut surfaces of the bread fingers with herb butter and place on baking sheet. Toast in very hot oven until golden brown. (Makes 24 fingers).

Salts For All Seasonings

Herb salts add flavor and zest to cookery and are a bonus for the diet conscious—the salt being diluted by the herb. Consequently, the body doesn't retain the extra fluid caused by too much salt intake.

While traveling in Europe, we found that herbs often take the place of our standby seasonings, salt and pepper. In salts as in other herb recipes, one must experiment to find the combinations preferred. We will give some of the basic recipes.

At least three herb salts can be made as a by-product when drying herbs by the salt method—chives, lovage and celery.

CHIVE SALT

After rinsing the chives in cold water, pat dry and snip into inch pieces. Put a layer of non-iodized salt on a cookie sheet, then a layer of chives, another layer of salt and another layer of chives. Place in oven at lowest temperature. It will take about 10 minutes for the chives to dry. Remove and sift. Store the dried chives in opaque jars. The salt which remains will contain little bits of chives and a lot of chive flavor. Use when you want the delicate taste of onion. Lovage and celery leaves may be dried the same way.

SPICED SALT

In this recipe you can use herbs which you have dried and prepared or herbs from the store.

Mix together 1½ teaspoons each of nutmeg, bay leaf, black pepper, powdered thyme. Add ¾ teaspoon of cayenne pepper and the same of marjoram and 3 teaspoons of powdered cloves. Sift these together and add 3 teaspoons salt. Keep in tightly closed cannister.

If you make this salt from your own herbs which have been dried and left in the leaf stage, powdering can be a tedious job. I crumble the leaves up as small as possible by hand and let the blender finish the job. The last step is to rub them through a fine sieve.

Spiced salt makes a good seasoning for stuffings, creamed dishes, poultry and meats.

HERB SALT NO. I

A basic herb salt that includes garlic calls for 1 cup salt, 2¼ teaspoons paprika, 1½ teaspoons ground ginger, ½ teaspoon white pepper, ¼ teaspoon mace, ¼ teaspoon thyme, ¼ teaspoon garlic salt. Stir together, put into well-corked cannister and shake.

HERB SALT NO. II

Combine 4 tablespoons salt, ½ tablespoon each—powdered thyme leaves, powdered marjoram, curry powder, powdered lovage leaves, 1 teaspoon each dry mustard and garlic salt and 2 teaspoons paprika. This salt is good with poultry.

PIQUANT SEASONING

Mix together 3 teaspoons each—powdered marjoram, powdered basil, powdered summer savory, thyme, 2 teaspoons each—powdered cloves, nutmeg, powdered chives, 1 bay leaf, 1 teaspoon grated lemon peel, ½ teaspoon cayenne pepper. Put in dry bottle and cork.

MOIST SALT

To make a moist salt with dill or fennel leaves, put a layer of non-iodized salt in bottom of jar. Alternately add leaves and salt in layers until jar is full, finishing with the salt. Seal tightly and let ripen two months.

CURRY POWDER

Combine 1 ounce each—ginger, coriander seed, cumin seed, cardamon seed, 3 ounces tumeric and ¼ ounce cayenne pepper.

A mixture of powdered herbs added to mayonnaise, sour cream or yogurt makes a good dressing for salad greens and a fine complement to the main dish. Here is another good recipe to try!

MINT CHUTNEY

In the electric blender, whirl together ¼ pound fresh mint leaves; 1 medium red onion, quartered; juice of one lime; 4 tablespoons chopped parsley; and ½ teaspoon chili powder. When this is blended, stir in 1 tablespoon sugar; 1 ½ teaspoons salt; ⅓ cup yogurt; and juice of a second lime.

Vinegar And Brown Paper-O

As a child I was stumped by the verse of "Jack and Jill," which went like this:

> "Up Jack got and home did trot,
> As fast as he could caper O.
> Went to bed and bound his head,
> With vinegar and brown paper O."

Years later I "got into herbs," and discovered the vinegar and brown paper combination was actually an old-time remedy for aches, bruises and contusions.

From old herbals we learn that pollution was around in the Elizabethan times—it was referred to as "noxious air." To mask unpleasant odors caused by unsanitary living conditions, court dandies and ladies carried intricate little silver balls called vinaigrettes. The silver containers had perforated tops and were filled with sponges soaked in aromatic vinegar.

Today we associate vinaigrette as a cold sauce or dressing made of vinegar and oil flavored with herbs.

Vinegar has long been used as a disinfecting agent. Perhaps leading up to this discovery was its effectiveness proven by an unusual source.

During the 18th century when a deadly plague swept through Paris, four thieves became notorious for entering homes of the dead and dying, stealing their possessions and escaping without catching the plague. Eventually the thieves were caught. The Court promised to let them go free if they would disclose the secret of their immunity. They "talked." It was a vinegar, they said, with which they bathed their faces and hands before entering the homes and with which they washed their clothing after an evening's foray. The recipe, passed down through the years, is still in use as a disinfectant, and aptly called "Vinegar of the Four Thieves."

VINEGAR OF THE FOUR THIEVES

Take a handful of each—lavender flowers, rosemary, sage, rue, wormwood and mint. Cover with 4 quarts of strong vinegar. Leave in a warm place to infuse for two weeks. Strain and add a clove of garlic to each bottle. When this settles in the bottle and becomes clear, pour off the liquid. Repeat process until no sediment remains. NOTE—never use metal containers or utensils when making vinegar. Use bottles with corks, glass lids or lids with a protective lining on glass, ceramic or stone jars.

AROMATIC VINEGAR

Bring 1 gallon cider vinegar to boiling point, add 1 ounce each—dill seed, lavender flowers, rue, spearmint, rosemary, sage, wormwood. Let stand in an earthen jar in warm place two weeks and strain.

SCENTED VINEGAR FOR DARK HAIR

Take 3 springs (two-inch tops from herb plant) fresh lavender flowers, rosemary or rose geranium and pour a pint of white vinegar which has been brought to the boiling point over them. Set the bottle in the sun and let the vinegar steep for 10 days. Strain through 3 thicknesses of cheesecloth. Use 1 tablespoon of the vinegar to a pint of water.

Scented vinegars are used to splash over one's face following a facial. The vinegar restores acidity to the skin. Very refreshing, too!

Gourmet vinegars are featured in many of the food speciality shops. The herb garden will provide the makings of many unusual flavors. This is another way the herbalist can experiment and come up with a special herbal product. The vinegars make appreciated gifts in this salad-conscious society.

Save salad dressing bottles, syrup bottles and shop for unusual jars and bottles in antique shops and flea markets for bottling your vinegars. Make an attractive label and include a note or folder with a recipe or two which uses the vinegar as an ingredient.

TARRAGON VINEGAR

Put 1 cup of washed fresh sprigs (two-inch tips) of a new growth of tarragon in a quart jar and pour white wine or cider vinegar which has been brought to a boiling point into the jar. Put on lid and shake the bottle before placing in the sun. I use a couple of bricks in the herb garden to hold the bottle. After 2 weeks, strain out the leaves through three thicknesses of cheesecloth, re-bottle and add a sprig of fresh tarragon before sealing.

BASIL VINEGAR

I prefer the dark opal basil because the resulting product is a lovely ruby color.

Strip the leaves from the basil stalks, wash and drain and pack loosely in a quart bottle. Pour hot white vinegar over the leaves and proceed as in above recipe.

Gerard says "the juice of sweet basil mixed with fine meal of parched barley, oil of roses and vinegar is good against inflammations and stinging of venomous beasts." It seems as though venomous beasts and noxious air were quite prevelant in his time, for he includes many herbs with virtues to combat the two.

A GARLIC VINEGAR

Garlic is added to many of the herb vinegars. This recipe dates back to the middle '80's.

Take 1 quart of white wine vinegar, the juice of 4 lemons, 6 cloves of garlic, half a nutmeg, and a few basil leaves; set the bottle in cool water; bring it to boiling heat. Cork tightly. It will take two or three drops to add the flavor to soups or sauces if desired. If the flavor of garlic is fairly discerned, it is disagreeable.

Burnet, marjoram, savory, thyme, mint, and rosemary vinegars are all prepared in the same way as the basil.

BORAGE VINEGAR

Pick the flowers of borage and put them into a wide-mouth jar filled with strong vinegar. Let this steep for three weeks, then strain, bottle and cork. The flavor is somewhat like cucumbers.

Lavender and Gilly Flowers (clove pinks) make delicate vinegars to use on fruit salads and are prepared the same as borage.

NASTURTIUM VINEGAR

Pick young nasturtium seeds and put them in vinegar. When all the strength is extracted, throw out the seeds and add more until the vinegar is very strongly flavored.

LEMON VINEGAR

Wash and dry 4 sprigs each of lemon basil, lemon balm, lemon thyme and 4 leaves of lemon verbena. Put these into a quart jar of white wine vinegar and add a thin spiral strip of lemon peel. Cure as in other processes.

SPECIAL MINT VINEGAR

Infuse 1 pint of bruised mint leaves and 1 cup of white sugar in a quart of cider vinegar for 24 hours. Use as a marinade or mint sauce. Use 2 tablespoons of mint vinegar, 2 tablespoons cream and 1 cup of mayonnaise for a fruit salad dressing.

SEED VINEGARS

A good vinegar to use in salads, such as potato and macaroni, is made with herb seeds. Drop a few dill, anise, caraway, cumin, coriander, sesame and cardamon seeds into a bottle of wine vinegar and let steep for 10 days. (Cardamon has a white outer shell so this must be removed and the tiny blacks seeds crushed). Strain through filter and re-bottle.

MUSTARD VINEGAR

Boil black mustard seed in strong vinegar until it is highly impregnated, then strain clear and bottle for use. Use in salad dressings which are to be made without thickening.

CHILI VINEGAR

Take 50 small ripe cayenne peppers, chop fine and infuse in a quart of cider vinegar for two weeks. Strain and bottle.

PEACH VINEGAR

Blanch 1 pint of peach pits by putting them in boiling water. Pour cold vinegar over them, as strong as can be obtained, and cork tightly.

Vinegar used in marinade gives tenderness and flavor to inexpensive cuts of meat.

A basic marinade mix is 12 tablespoons oil, 3 tablespoons vinegar, ¼ teaspoon pepper, 1 teaspoon salt. Add choice of herb in the ratio of ½ teaspoon.

BASIC MARINADE

Mix together ½ cup olive oil, 3 tablespoons lemon juice, 6 tablespoons tarragon vinegar, 1 teaspoon salt, 1 clove garlic or 3 cloves shallots, a grind of black pepper. Put into blender and then pour over hot vegetables.

STEW MARINADE

Combine 1 tablespoon cider vinegar, ⅓ cup vegetable oil, small bay leaf (crumbled), 1½ teaspoons salt, ¼ teaspoon marjoram, ½ teaspoon thyme leaves, 1½ teaspoon minced shallots, ½ teaspoon garlic salt and 2 tablespoons lemon juice.

POULTRY MARINADE (*for salt-free diet*)

Combine ½ cup white wine vinegar, one sprig each—parsley, orange mint, rosemary, marjoram, tarragon and lemon thyme. Rub bird with cooking oil then pour over the wine mixture. Put into plastic bag and keep refrigerated overnight (Can be used with frozen bird).

CHICKEN MARINADE

Put cut-up chicken in shallow pan and pour over a marinade made of ⅔ cup vegetable oil, 1 teaspoon regular salt, 1 teaspoon spiced salt, ¼ teaspoon tarragon, 2 tablespoons chopped parsley, grind of pepper.

Soup's On!

A lot can be said for a kettle of soup, whether it be a hearty pot-au-feu or delicate consomme—and the right herbs can help "say" it.

Let's begin with the French bouquet garni. This usually consists of three herbs or more, tied together with a string for easy removal from the soup before serving.

A basic bouquet garni is a sprig of parsley, a sprig of thyme, and a sprig of lovage or celery leaves.

A more complicated garni is 1 sprig each of parsley, summer savory, chervil, basil, 1 stalk celery with leaves and 6 chive leaves.

Bouquet garni for tomato soup—1 sprig each of parsley and basil, small onion and bay leaf.

Bouquet garni for pea soups—1 sprig each of rosemary, lovage and parsley.

DRIED HERB BOUQUET

Combine ½ cup dried parsley flakes, ¼ cup thyme leaves. Divide into three bags (2-inch square cheesecloth) and add ¼ bay leaf and 1 peppercorn to each bag.

FRESH HERB BOUQUET

Combine 3 sprigs parsley, 2 sprigs thyme, 1 bay leaf. For seafood add 2 sprigs of tarragon; for poultry add a sprig of rosemary or marjoram; for tomato add a sprig of basil and for beans add 2 sprigs of summer savory, 3 chive leaves and 1 sprig thyme.

SOUP BAGS

Cut muslin or double thickness of cheesecloth into 3-inch squares and divide the following mixture: ¼ teaspoon peppercorns, 2 teaspoons thyme, 1 teaspoon marjoram, 5 teaspoons parsley, ½ teaspoon summer savory, 3 tablespoons lovage and one clove to each bag. Tie with string. One bag will season 2 quarts of liquid and should be added to the boiling soup the last 20 minutes of cooking.

VICHYSOISSE NO. I

Sauté 1½ cup of minced leeks (the white portion) and one medium onion chopped in 2 tablespoons margarine or butter. Add 3 cups boiling water in which 4 chicken boullion cubes have been dissolved, 2 cups of potatoes peeled and thinly sliced, 2 peppercorns, ¼ cup of chopped celery (or 1 stalk of lovage and leaves, chopped). When potatoes are mushy, put soup in blender or through ricer. Stir in 1 cup of half and half and 1 teaspoon salt. Cool and chill. Serve in bowls and garnish with chopped fresh chives.

VICHYSOISSE NO. II

Sauté 4 leeks and 1 thinly sliced onion in 2 tablespoons butter. Add to 4 medium potatoes peeled and diced, 1 stalk celery, 2 peppercorns and salt to taste. Put in kettle with water to cover and cook until mushy. Add a can of cream of chicken soup, bring to boil and put in blender. Chill. Before serving, add 1 cup of cream and sprinkle chopped chives over each serving.

QUICK POTATO SOUP

Whenever I fix mashed potatoes I always make some extra to use in this quick soup. I also save the potato water.

Sauté a small chopped onion, stalk celery and leaves (chopped), in a little margarine. Add a cup of potato water and when the celery is tender, stir in the left-over mashed potatoes. You may need to add a little more potato water. Heat to boiling point. Thin with a little milk or cream and add several sprigs of fresh parsley (chopped) or 2 tablespoons of dried parsley flakes. If you have lovage, the leaves will give extra flavor and don't forget a grind of fresh pepper. A Greek friend always adds a little fresh lemon juice to potato soup.

VEGETABLE-BEEF SOUP

Put into large kettle 2 pounds of boiling beef, a soup bone, 2 tablespoons salt and 2 quarts of water. Bring to boiling point, turn fire to simmer and cook 3 hours. Skim off scum, remove bone and chop the meat into small pieces. Add to broth and meat 1 cup sliced celery, 1 cup sliced carrots, 1 chopped onion, 1 cup of fresh or canned corn, 1 turnip and 2 diced potatoes, 1 cup of fresh lima beans, 1 cup green beans, 1 quart of strained tomatoes, a handful of fresh chopped parsley. (Add potatoes last). Sometimes I put in 2 tablespoons of rice or barley. Cook until vegetables are almost tender then add 2 soup bags. Left over soup can be frozen, better still—share it with a neighbor. Makes one gallon of soup.

BEAN SOUP

Wash and drain 1 cup of navy beans. Put into kettle with 2 quarts of cold water and a ham bone or ham hock. Bring to boil, reduce heat and place on cover. Simmer beans until tender. When beans are half-cooked, add 1 tablespoon salt, 1 small onion, ¼ cup chopped celery, including leaves and 2 sprigs summer savory. Remove savory before serving.

SPLIT PEA OR LENTIL SOUP

Wash and soak overnight 1½ cups of dried split peas or lentils. Drain. Put into kettle with 3 quarts of water, a ham bone, a medium onion (chopped), 2 carrots, peeled and sliced. Salt to season, add two peppercorns. Cook over low heat (about 3 hours) until peas are mushy. Remove ham bone and dice the bits of meat to add to soup after the soup has been put through a ricer. Also add ½ teaspoon marjoram, a tablespoon of margarine and 2 cups of milk. Heat thoroughly. (Very rich).

Tisane Anyone?

Healthful-Fragrant-Delicious are words to describe herb teas, however, the French have another word for them—tisanes.

Always popular on the continent, herb teas really gained prominence during the Revolutionary War when the colonists found it necessary to substitute for imported tea. Their ingenuity triumphed and we are enjoying some of their discoveries today. They experimented with many plants and called the products Liberty Teas.

If you've never tried wild strawberry, wild blackberry or wild red raspberry tea, you've missed a treat. The aroma and flavor are so fragrant you'll imagine yourself in a sun-drenched berry field. To give the berry leaves a semblance of the imported tea, the housewife would roll the leaves and let them dry.

There are several rules one should observe to get the most from brewing a tisane. First—do not expect the tea to be dark in color. Most herbal teas are pale green or light golden. Second—always use a porcelin or ceramic pot. Pour the boiling water over the herb and allow to steep for 5 to 15 minutes. (Time will vary). The proportion of tea to use—1 teaspoon of the dried leaves or flowers to 1 cup of water. If fresh herbs are used, make it 2 teaspoons. Sometimes lemon juice is added and the tea may be sweetened with honey.

Medicinal virtues are ascribed to many of the herb teas. For example: camomile tea soothes the stomach and induces sleep; peppermint settles the stomach; sage tea and lavender tea are supposed to alleviate headaches; ginger tea warms the stomach; tansy tea was given to alleviate the pains of childbirth; boneset and sassafras teas were given as spring tonics. Boneset is very bitter, but the sassafras tea is delicious. The bark must be scrubbed, placed in cold water and allowed to simmer for about 15 minutes. It fills the kitchen with a delightful fragrance when it is brewing.

Usually a taste for herb teas must be acquired. One may begin by adding a mint leaf, rose geranium, peppermint geranium or lemon verbena leaf to a cup of regular hot tea. Somehow the tea always tastes better if served in dainty porcelin cups.

CAMOMILE TEA

The daisy-like flowers are used for this tea which is very popular in Europe, especially in Germany. Use 1 teaspoon to a pint of boiling water and let steep 5 to 10 minutes in a covered teapot. Pour through strainer and sweeten with honey.

CRIMSON TEA

Mix dried ingredients in following proportions: 5 parts red rose petals to 1 part rosemary leaves and two parts rose geranium leaves. Allow 1 teaspoon of the mixture to 1 cup of boiling water. Infuse 5 minutes.

Comfrey, peppermint, orange mint, sage, sweet woodruff, costmary, dried and used separately or in a combination will make refreshing teas. Experimenting with various combinations is one of the ways an herbalist can be inventive. Who knows, you may come up with a prize-winning brew!

One can also make herbal teas from seeds and roots. A

combination of herb seeds calls for equal proportions of caraway, coriander, fennel and aniseed.

Sage tea is bitter and will have a better taste if diluted with some lemon or orange rind and the addition of sugar. This tea is credited with many virtues. According to the French saying: "Sage helps the nerves and by its powerful might, Palsy is cured and fever put to flight."

Horehound tea is used for coughs and sore throat. It, too, is bitter, but honey added improves the taste.

CUB SCOUT TEA

This is actually regular tea with mint added, but we dubbed it Cub Scout Tea because our cubscouts always expected it after a den meeting. The tea became so popular at our house that the little neighbor boy who mowed our lawn insisted on a glass of tea as part of his pay. He never forgot it and when he returned home from college and became engaged, he brought his fiancee to the house and asked me to make her "some of that tea."

To make two quarts, put 5 tea bags and a handful of fresh mint leaves into a small saucepan and add 1 cup of water. Bring to boil (this releases the volatile oil in the mint). Remove from heat and add 2 cups of cold water. Strain into pitcher and sweeten. Finish filling the pitcher with cracked ice. This will make 5 glasses.

Herbal teas do not introduce poisonous chemicals into the body such as caffeine or tannic acids. They do introduce valuable elements to the human system—both nutritional and healing qualities. They are non-habit forming and children may drink them, so do try a tisane!

Can It!

Preserve that wonderful flavor of herbs when they are at the peak of their freshness—straight from the garden, by canning. Use in pickles, vegetables, relishes, jellies and conserves.

Some of the most used herbs in canning are dill, mint, garlic, horseradish, rose geranium and basil.

Let's begin with the jellies. Here the herbalist can have a ball coming up with jellies that look like jewels, are delicately flavored and delightful for giving.

Some people are natural jelly makers—the juice jells at the right moment with the jelly clear and livery. My mother is a jelly maker and there were times when pectin was not available and she would stand patiently over a steaming kettle of blackberry juice and sugar waiting for the right moment. She tested with a metal spoon. When the liquid stopped flowing from the spoon in a stream and divided into two distinct drops which ran together and left the edge of the spoon in one large flake, she knew the jelly was ready to pour. In our recipes we will be making jelly by the quicker method—using a fruit pectin. Mint grew abundantly in our garden and was one of mom's favorites. Her recipe follows:

MOM'S MINT JELLY

1 ½ packed cups of fresh mint
3 ¼ cups water
1 box fruit pectin
4 cups sugar

Crush the mint leaves and stems. Add 3 ¼ cups water and bring to boil. Remove from heat, cover and let infuse for 10 minutes. Strain and measure 3 cups of the mint infusion and add just a few drops of green food coloring to tint. Mix pectin with juice in a large sauce pan and, over high heat, quickly bring mixture to rolling boil, stirring constantly. At once, add sugar. Bring to rolling boil and boil hard 1 minute, stirring constantly. Remove from heat and skim off foam. Pour at once into sterile glasses, leaving ½ inch space at top. This makes 4 ½ cups of jelly.

WILD MINT WITH APPLE

4 cups of apple juice
1 box fruit pectin
6 drops green food coloring
1 cup fresh mint leaves (lightly packed)
4 ½ cups sugar

Combine apple juice, pectin, food coloring and mint leaves in a very large kettle. Bring to hard boil and boil hard for 2 minutes, stirring constantly. Remove from heat and take out the mint leaves. Pour into hot scalded jars. Seal. Makes 6 half-pint jars.

When we were children, my brothers and I liked to visit a spinster lady who lived a mile below town. She looked like a little ante-bellum doll and wore her grey hair in finger curls. Her cottage was down over the hill from the highway and surrounded by cherry trees. She called her little farm "Cherry Dale," and I remember she wrote and sent gifts to all the Republican presidents, was proud of being a descendent of "The Calverts" and the only daughter of a Civil War veteran to receive a pension. She raised chickens and named them after people she liked. On one of our visits she was making a batch of apple jelly. The jelly was pale brown and she placed a rose of geranium leaf in each glass. At the time I thought it a bit weird, but when we got home with our sample glass of jelly we wasted no time in trying it out on homemade bread and found it delicious.

I make it now for my own family, but for the base I like to use crab apples since it makes a beautiful pink jelly.

CRAB APPLE JELLY WITH ROSE GERANIUM LEAVES

> 7 cups of prepared crab apple juice
> 9 cups sugar
> 1 box fruit pectin
> rose geranium leaves

Remove blossom and stem ends from fully ripe, tart crab apples; cut in half (do not peel or core). Add 5 cups of water and simmer covered, 10 minutes. Crush with masher and simmer 5 minutes longer. Place in jelly bag and squeeze. (For a clear, sparkling jelly let the juice drip overnight.) Mix pectin with juice in saucepan, quickly bring to hard boil and add sugar. Bring to full rolling boil and boil hard 3 minutes, stirring constantly. Remove from heat, skim off foam with metal spoon. Pour at once into sterile jars into which you have previously placed a rose geranium leaf. Makes 10 cups of jelly. Serve with pork and poultry.

Now for some variations using the crab apple juice for the base. Instead of using the rose geranium, try a leaf of opal basil, pineapple sage, a lemon verbena leaf or even a carnation pink (the English gillyfower) in a glass.

BASIL JELLY I

I raise both green bush basil and opal basil, but for this recipe I prefer the green basil.

1 cup fresh green basil leaves packed tightly
½ box of fruit pectin
few drops green coloring
1 ½ cups sugar
1 ¾ cups water
2 tablespoons lemon juice

Boil the basil leaves in the water for 3 minutes, strain and add 3 drops of green food coloring and the lemon juice (vinegar may be substituted). Add sugar and pectin and bring to a full rolling boil and maintian for 1 minute, stirring constantly. Put a leaf of basil in the bottom of the sterilized glass and pour in hot jelly. Seal.

BASIL JELLY WITH TOMATO

1 cup opal basil leaves packed tightly
2 cups of tomato juice
1 ½ cups sugar
½ box pectin

Boil basil leaves in tomato juice for 3 minutes and strain. Stir in sugar and pectin and bring to boil. Keep at rolling boil 1 minute, skim. Place a basil leaf in the bottom of each sterilized glass and pour in jelly. Seal. Good with meatloaf.

ROSEMARY JELLY

2 cans (6 oz. each) orange concentrate (thawed),
    plus 2 ½ cups water
1 box pectin
4 ½ cups sugar
orange peel
4 sprigs (two-inch strips) rosemary tied in cheesecloth bag,
    plus tiny sprigs for each glass.

Mix pectin, orange juice, water and rosemary in large kettle. Stir constantly over high heat until bubbles form around edge. Remove rosemary. At once add sugar and stir. Bring to full rolling boil and boil hard for 1 minute. Stir constantly. Remove from heat, skim and pour into sterile jars. Add one tiny sprig of rosemary and a sliver of orange peel to each jar.

THYME-GRAPE JELLY

1 cup thyme washed well and drained
7 cups sugar
5 cups grape juice
1 box pectin

Boil thyme in grape juice and strain. Add sugar, pectin, and proceed as in other recipes.

VIOLET OR ROSE PETAL JELLY

4 cups of violet or rose petals, the white heels clipped out
3¼ cups boiling water
3¼ cups sugar
1 box fruit pectin
1 tablespoon lemon juice

Use strong colored petals—deep purple violets or deep red rose petals (Crimson Glory is my choice). Put the petals in a big bowl and cover with the boiling water. Let rose petals stand 30 minutes, but leave the violets overnight. Strain into kettle and add sugar. Bring to rolling boil, add pectin and lemon juice and again bring to a rolling boil. Boil for 1 minute more, then skim. The violet juice will turn a beautiful shade of violet when the lemon juice is added. Pour into sterilized jars and seal.

You can make the herb jellies even more interesting by clever packaging. I sometimes use tiny little jars that pimientoes come in and paint the lids white and make a tiny painting of the herb in the center of the lid. Use a thin layer of paraffin on top of the jelly before putting on the lid. The lids may be covered with calico or gingham. The attractive half-pint jars on the market are also nice to use.

RHUBARB JELLY

Rhubarb is one of the spring tonic herbs. Not only is it refreshing stewed and in pies, it makes an unusual and delicious jelly. Angelica leaves or some of the tender angelica stalks can be added for extra flavor. Cook rhubarb, covered with water, until color leaves it. Drain. To 4 cups rhubarb juice add 1 box fruit pectin. Put into large kettle and cook to a full rolling boil. At once (stirring constantly) add 4 cups of sugar. Bring to full boil. Cook 1 minute. Remove from heat, skim and pour into hot jelly jars. A few drops of red coloring may be added.

CONSERVE OF FLOWERS

Recipes from old herbals use equal amounts of petals and sugar. Pound them together, add a little water and cook until thick. Pot marigold conserve was a favorite of Gerard, who said: ''a conserve made of the marigold flowers and sugar and taken in the morning fasting cureth the trembling of the heart; and is also given in time of plague or pestilence, or corruption of the aire.''

To make the Pot Marigold conserve, use 1 cup of petals and 1 cup of sugar. Boil until this begins to thicken and add 1 tablespoon of lemon juice. Pour into sterilized jar (makes about ½ pint). A tablespoon of the conserve is soothing to sore throats and if you are making some fancy cookies, try the Thumbprint cookie recipe and fill the center with the marigold conserve.

CANNING VEGETABLES

A short-cut to seasoning vegetables is to add the herb to the vegetable before the canning process. To a quart of tomatoes put two springs of basil, plus salt and ½ teaspoon sugar. To a quart of green beans add two sprigs of summer savory. To a pint of peas add a sprig of fresh mint. To a pint of beets put a sprig of tarragon or a sliver of horseradish (do not add to pickled beets). In canning soup, be generous with basil, oregano, thyme and parsley.

PICKLES

Much advice has been given on how to make pickles crisp and green. Some say to be sure the vinegar is strong and to never use metal kettles, spoons, etc.

To keep the pickles a nice shade of green, one can steep parsley or spinach in hot vinegar, strain and add to pickles. A grape leaf placed in the bottom of each jar of pickles is supposed to prevent the pickles from becoming soft. To clarify pickles, add some horseradish root. Now for some recipes.

DILL PICKLES

> 25 (4-inch) cucumbers
> dill, garlic cloves, powdered alum
> 1 cup coarse salt
> 1 quart cider vinegar
> 3 quarts water

Let cucumbers stand in cold water overnight. Pack in hot sterilized jars. Add 2 teaspoons dill (sprigs of green seed head), 1 clove garlic and 1/8 teaspoon alum to each jar. Combine salt, 3 quarts of water and vinegar. Heat to boiling point. Fill jars with hot liquid and seal. Yield is 6-8 quarts.

CRISP PICKLE SLICES

> 4 quarts sliced cucumbers
> 2 green peppers (chopped)

½ cup coarse salt
½ teaspoon tumeric
2 tablespoons mustard seed
6 medium sliced onions
3 cloves garlic
5 cups sugar
1½ teaspoons celery seed
3 cups cider vinegar

Put cucumber slices, onions, pepper and whole garlic in pan. Add salt, mix thoroughly. Cover with cracked ice. Cover and let stand for 3 hours. Drain. Combine remaining ingredients, pour over cucumbers. Heat just to boil. Seal in hot jars. Yield is 8 pints.

LIME PICKLES

First day—wash and slice 1½ gallons cucumbers. Mix 2 cups lime in 2 gallons water, cover cucumbers and let stand for 24 hours.

Second day—drain off liquid and rinse at least 3 times in very cold water. Cover with clear water and let stand 3 hours. Drain water off. Mix 2 quarts vinegar, 9 cups sugar, 1 tablespoon salt, 1 teaspoon celery seed, 1 tablespoon pickling spices, 1 teaspoon whole cloves. Tie all spices in white cloth. Let stand overnight in this mixture with cucumbers.

Third day—boil pickles 4 or 5 minutes in this mixture. Pour into jars and seal. Yields about 12 pints.

CRYSTAL PICKLES (sweet)

Into clean stone jar put 2 gallons of cucumbers (about 24) washed and cut into chunks. Dissolve 2 cups of coarse salt in 1 gallon of boiling water and pour while hot over the cucumbers. Then cover and weight down pickles and let stand for 1 week. Remove scum daily. On the 8th day, drain, then pour 1 gallon of boiling water over them (to which you add 1 tablespoon alum). Make fresh water with alum each day and repeat process for 4 days.

For the pickling mixture combine 6 cups vinegar, 5 cups sugar, ⅓ cup pickling spices and 1 tablespoon celery seed. Bring to boil and pour this over the pickles. The 12th day, drain and save liquid, add 2 cups sugar, bring to boil and pour over pickles. On the 13th day, add 1 cup of sugar and repeat process. On the 14th day, heat and pack pickles in sterilized jars to within ½ inch of jar top. Put on cap, screw band firmly tight. Process in boiling water bath for 60 minutes.

ICE PICKLES

> 1 heaped gallon pickles (sliced)
> 3 cut-up medium mangoes
> 6 medium onions (sliced)
> ⅓ cup salt

Put above ingredients into bowl and cover with ice. Let stand for 4 hours, then drain pickles.

Mix together 5 cups sugar, 3 cups vinegar, 1 tablespoon whole mustard seed, 1 tablespoon whole celery seed and 1 tablespoon tumeric. Bring to full rolling boil. Put pickle mixture in it and bring to full boil again. Put into jars and seal.

ZUCCHINI PICKLES

> 2 pounds small zucchini
> ¼ cup salt
> 1 cup sugar
> ½ teaspoon powdered mustard
> 2 medium onions
> 2 cups white vinegar
> 1 teaspoon each—celery seed and ground tumeric

Wash zucchini. Cut unpeeled zucchini and peeled onion into very thin slices and drop into crock or bowl. Cover with water and add salt. Let stand 1 hour and drain. Mix remaining ingredients and bring to boil. Pour over zucchini and onions. Let stand 1 hour. Put in kettle and bring to boil and cook 3 minutes. Pack into sterilized jars and seal. Yield is 3 pints.

BREAD AND BUTTER PICKLES

Mix ⅓ cup coarse salt with 4 quarts sliced cucumbers (small ones are best), 6 medium sliced onions, 2 chopped green peppers. Let stand 3 hours with ice cubes and 3 cloves garlic. Drain and discard garlic. Mix 3 cups sugar, 3 cups vinegar, 2 tablespoons mustard seed, 1½ teaspoons of both celery seed and tumeric. Let come to boil, add pickles; let come to boil again and seal in sterilized jars.

GREEN TOMATO RELISH

     8 cups chopped green tomatoes
     2 sweet peppers (chopped)
     2 cups chopped onion
Salt vegetables and let stand 1 hour. Boil the following a few minutes: 2 cups vinegar, 2 sticks cinnamon, 2 cups sugar, 2 teaspoons tumeric. Add vegetables. Bring to boil and seal in jars.

CORN RELISH

     2 quarts corn (about 18 ears)
     1 cup sweet green peppers
     2 large onions
     1 cup sugar
     1 quart vinegar
     1 tablespoon salt
     1 quart cabbage (half a head)
     1 cup red sweet peppers or pimientoes
     2 tablespoons ground mustard
     1 tablespoon mustard seed
     1 cup water
Boil corn 5 minutes, cold dip. Cut from cob but do not scrape. Measure. Chop and measure cabbage and peppers. Chop onions. Combine ingredients and simmer 10 minutes (more salt and sugar may be added if needed). Pack into sterile jars and seal. This recipe takes about 2 hours to make and is one of the old-time Pennsylvania Dutch Sweets and Sours. It is good with fried potatoes.

END OF GARDEN SALAD

Soak 1 cup sliced cucumbers, 1 cup peppers, 1 cup chopped cabbage, 1 cup sliced onions and 1 cup chopped green tomatoes in salt overnight (½ cup salt to 2 quarts water). Drain. Cook 1 cup chopped carrots and 1 cup green string beans in boiling water until tender. Drain well. Mix soaked and cooked vegetables with the following: 2 tablespoons mustard seed, 1 tablespoon celery seed, 1 cup chopped celery, 2 cups sugar, 2 cups vinegar and 2 tablespoons tumeric. Cook at boiling point 10 minutes. Pack into jars and seal.

INDIA RELISH (A good item at bazaars)

½ peck green tomatoes
16 sweet peppers (part green and part red)
2 pounds sugar
3 pints vinegar
2 tablespoons allspice
2 tablespoons whole cloves
2 tablespoons cinnamon bark
2 large onions
1 tablespoon celery seed
2 tablespoons whole white mustard seed
2 tablespoons salt

Tie spices in bag. Put tomatoes, peppers and onions through coarse blade of chopper. Boil 15 minutes and drain. Add vinegar, sugar and spices and cook 10 minutes. Add the pickle ingredients and salt. Bring to boil. Seal in hot sterile jars.

BEET RELISH

This recipe calls for horseradish (recipe for this is in "Granny's in the Kitchen"). To 4 cups of ground cooked beets and 4 cups of ground cabbage add ½ cup prepared horseradish, 1 cup sugar, 1 tablespoon salt. Put into hot sterile jars and cover with hot vinegar. Seal. Always keep beets protected from light.

MOM'S SANDWICH SPREAD

During the Depression years, this surely tasted good on mom's homemade bread.

Grind 18 red and 18 sweet peppers, 6 onions, 6 green tomatoes. Cover with boiling water and let stand 10 minutes. Drain well. Add 3 cups vinegar, 1½ cups brown sugar, 2 tablespoons salt and cook 8 minutes. Blend 3 tablespoons dry mustard with 6 tablespoons flour and enough water to make a thin paste. Add to above ingredients and boil until thickened. Add 1 quart of mayonnaise and cook until heated. Put into sterilized jars and seal.

RUBY'S SANDWICH SPREAD

Grind fine and drain 6 large red peppers, 6 large green peppers and 3 medium onions,

Cook: 1 cup sugar, 1 cup vinegar, ¾ cup mustard, 1 cup butter, ¼ cup flour and salt to taste. Mix the flour and sugar, stir into other ingredients. Now add the vegetables and cook 15 minutes. Seal in hot sterilized jars.

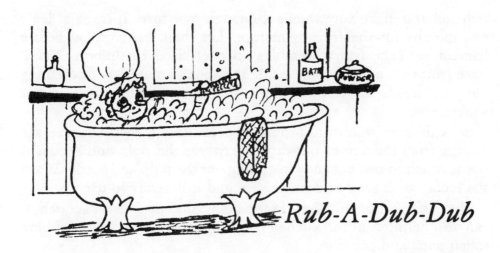

Rub-A-Dub-Dub

That siren of the Nile, Cleopatra, will have nothing on you if you take advantage of those magic herbs in your garden. In fact, if the lighting is good and you have the space, you can hang a basket of thyme, mint, rosemary and lemon verbena in the bathroom. Then all you will need to do is take a handful, put them in an old nylon stocking and hang it over the faucet—instant herbal bath!

A rather recent beauty aid we are growing in this country is the luffa or loofah sponge. The plant originated in India some 2000 years ago and practically every bathroom in England has a loofah sponge harking back to the days when they were imported from India.

There is a story dating back 500 years about a Korean king who ordered his men to find a sponge strong enough to cleanse his body yet gentle enough not to scratch his skin. The men came up with Susem (the Korean name for loofah). He decreed loofah should become the royal bath sponge. The Japanese and Europeans later adopted it.

Some doctors recommend the loofah for removing dry, flaky skin and to stimulate blood circulation.

The loofah is a long season crop, so the seeds should be started indoors in early spring and transplanted when the ground is warm. It is a vine and needs support. Set the plants about 2 inches apart in rich soil and make sure they get enough moisture. İt takes at least two months for the fruit to mature. Let them turn yellow before harvesting. (The fruit resembles an over-sized cucumber). You'll have fruit with a fleshy part inside the spongy material—something like the inside of a pumpkin, with black seeds much like a watermelon.

Soak them in water until the skin peels easily, then squeeze the sponge from the center outward to remove the pulp and seeds. A bottle brush comes in handy in getting out the pulp and seeds. Wash the loofah with soap and water, dry and it is ready to use.

The loofah is not only good in the bath. Since it doesn't scratch, it can also help out in the kitchen. It is especially good for scrubbing teflon pans and porcelin.

After the loofahs are dry, you can cut them into small sponges, leave whole or make bath mitts.

To make a mitt, trace a pattern of your hand, leaving an extra inch all around. Split a large loofah and lay it over a piece of terry cloth and cut out. Bind the two pieces together with bias tape, leaving a small loop on one corner so the mitt may be hung up to dry.

BATH BAGS

Mints, bergamot, thymes, rosemary, lavender, comfrey, sweet marjoram, and rose petals all make refreshing bath bags.

According to old herbals, bergamot was used by knights of old as a rubdown after a bout of jousting. This supposedly eased the muscles and, when followed by a warm bath containing bergamot, it "soothed the nerves and strengthened the sinews."

Remove the leaves from the dried plants and use singly or combine any of the above. Cut the bags from muslin into 3-½ inch squares. To get the most benefit from them, steep the bags in boiling water for 5 minutes and then add the water to the bath.

A set of 6 bath bags using different combinations and tied with a colorful ribbon makes a nice gift.

BATH SALTS

It's not only easy, but also fun to make your own bath salts. Combine 2 cups of Epsom salts with 6 drops of lavender oil and a few drops of violet food coloring.

For rose bath salts, add rose geranium oil and a drop or two of red food coloring. With bergamot oil, add green coloring.

Another recipe calls for 6 ounces of bicarbonate of soda, 6 ounces of tartaric acid and 4 ounces of cornstarch. Crush and mix in mortar. If you are not allergic to orris root, it can be used instead of the cornstarch. Add any favorite herb oil for scent.

SOAPS

A little time and patience and you can make some delightfully fragrant and really good cleansing soaps in your own kitchen. Have ready some of the equipment before you begin—molds for instance. If you want to cut the soap into bars later, line a wooden box about 14 inches square (you may have to make it) and soak it in cold water for half an hour. Line the box with a square of muslin also dampened. Individual candle molds make attractive shapes. I like the little angel and flower molds. These should be sprayed with a non-stick pan coater. Put out papers to protect working surfaces and on the floor around the stove, just in case you might spill some of the soap. Now begin.

Melt a 3 pound can of inexpensive shortening over a low flame. Cool to about 90 degrees. Meantime dissolve half a can household lye (about 7 ounces) in 2½ cups of cold water. Stir with a stainless steel knife or spoon and be sure to use a stainless steel bowl or pan (*Never* plastic or aluminum). Mix it thoroughly. Let it cool out of reach of children. This will take about half an hour.

Add fragrant oil of your choice (rose, lavender, bergamot, lemon verbena) to the shortening and a wafer or two of candle coloring to correspond to the fragrance.

Pour the lye mixture slowly into the shortening, stirring gently with a wooden spoon—always stir in the same direction. (Add the lye as you do syrup to egg white when making divinity—in a steady stream).

Keep stirring in the same circular direction for 5 minutes after you have added all the liquid, then let it rest for 15 minutes, only stirring it occasionally. It thickens gradually. When it resembles a thick sauce, pour it into the molds. Work quickly as it sets up like fudge. Cover the molds with a sheet of heavy paper or several layers of newspapers and add an old rug to hold in the heat. It should cure slowly. Don't disturb the molds for 2 days. After this, you can store it somewhere to age. The soap in the box may be cut into bars after about 3 days, Return them to the box to harden.

You can use strong herbal teas to scent your soap. In this case, substitute the tea for part of the cold water used to dissolve the dye. Natural coloring such as beet juice, spinach juice or marigold juice will give a soft color. Be sure to allow how much of this is used when measuring the water.

These soaps are nice to scent linen closets and would be pretty and fragrant in a little basket in the bathroom. The cakes of soap can be wrapped in colorful calico or gingham and given as gifts.

Herbs makes excellent astringents and the following recipe provides a refreshing facial.

Squeeze the juice of a lemon, strain into 1 pint of water and add 3 sprigs of fresh rosemary. Keep refrigerated when not in use. This is the astringent.

The cleanser is made with raw oatmeal powdered in the electric blender. Wash the face and splash on hot water, then dip fingertips into the oatmeal and rub into the pores of the face. Rub until the face feels dry and smooth. Splash on more hot water and as a final rinse use the astringent. The lemon juice restores the acidity to the skin and the rosemary tightens the pores.

Let Herbs Say A Fragrant "Hello"

It is always nice to hear guests ask: "Mmmmm, what is that delightful fragrance!" when they enter your home. The answer—if you are an herbalist—"just some herbs." Of course, when one is expecting company, it doesn't do any harm to have herb bread or spice cookies baking in the oven.

There are many ways to use herbs in giving fragrance to every room in the house. Let's start at the top—the attic. Here we have aromatic herbs hanging to dry on lines strung from the rafters. More fragile herbs are spread out on screens. Small muslin bags filled with aromatic moth repellents are tucked into clothing and storage boxes. Sweet woodruff, that delightful herb which emanates a perfume much like that of new mown hay, may be strewn in trunks. All of these herbs will dispel the mustiness which is synonomous with attics and many will also help repel insects harmful to clothing.

In second floor bedrooms the fragrance choice of the occupant hold sway. Perhaps the son of the house prefers a woodsy odor; the daughter, a spicy fragrance; dad may like the clean smell of lavender, while mom goes for lemon verbena. Potpourri and sachets may be made up in the choice scent to perfume dresser drawers, clothes closets, bed linens and bathrooms.

Making matched accessories for the bedroom is a clever gift idea. Just carry out the decorating accent; country style with crosspatch; Early American with calico; Victorian with damask and lace, etc. Directions are simple.

A padded clothes hanger—trace around a wire coat hanger for your pattern. Cut 2 thicknesses of material and 2 thicknesses of thin cotton or other lightweight batting. A wide choice of printed and plain materials comes already quilted. If you use these, omit batting.

Stitch the curved top, leaving a very small opening for the hanger. Insert the hanger and fill with dry potpourri mixture (about a cup full). Stitch across bottom. The edges may be pinked or bound. Close the opening at the top and camouflage with a ribbon, bow or other trimming.

Padded Hanger

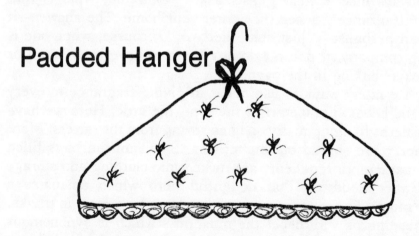

Scented linings for dresser drawers are always appreciated. Make a pattern to fit the drawer, cut 2 thicknesses of the material and 2 of the batting. Put a thin layer of potpourri between the batting layers and pin so they won't slide when you sew around the edges. Bind with tape or leave a stitching margin around the lining so it can be pinked.

Dresser Drawer Liner

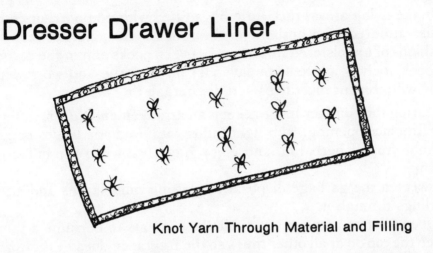

Knot Yarn Through Material and Filling

Cases for hosiery, lingerie, hankies and gloves are envelope style and can be made in the same manner.

For the beginner, an easy choice is plain, unbleached muslin. Trim with contrasting color (ribbon, bias binding or yarn using a blanket stitch). Tie the lining together with yarn knots like the comforters grandmother used to make.

Fancier sachets to place among sweaters, hang in the press and carry in one's purse are filled with sachet (potpourri ground into a fine powder). Patterns for some of these are included in this chapter.

The Victorian shoe, made from nylon velvet and trimmed with lace, buttons, beads and a buckle of discarded jewelry (one way to use up lone earrings) and filled with lavender will scent a closet. Other sachets include the Granny Lavender and Rosy "heads," panties, Santa boot and mitten. The small sachets make clever little favors and are nice to tuck into a get-well or birthday card.

Sweet bags for the linen closet can be made in different fragrances too. Lavender alone is excellent, so are costmary and the scented geraniums. A pleasing combination is lavender flowers, pineapple sage, balm, sweet marjoram, coriander, lemon verbena, whole cloves and bay leaf. Put into muslin bags 3 x 6 inches or larger.

In the living areas, tuck little bags filled with potpourri or cotton balls saturated with herbal oils or aromatic vinegars between the cushions of upholstered furniture. Between books and in the corners of book shelves, place some lavender flowers, rue and wormwood. This will prevent mustiness and discourage tiny insects.

During the summer months keep an arrangement of fresh mint in the fireplace opening. Rub light bulbs with aromatic leaves or give them a drop of herbal oil and enjoy fragrance when the bulbs get warm.

Sweeten the garbage disposal by putting mint leaves and citrus peelings through it.

Open a jar of potpourri and stir the contents to perfume a room. Keep the top on at all other times so the fragrance doesn't dissipate.

To leave tile floors and cupboard shelves with a pleasant scent and at the same time discourage fleas, moths, ants, spiders and other insect pests, scrub with a brew of strong herbal tea using mint, basil, southernwood, tansy, clove pinks, sweet marjoram, lavender flowers, or rosemary; a combination or any herb singly.

Even your sweeper can join in refreshing your house! Sprinkle some herbal oil, some of the above tea or aromatic vinegar on the filter. As the sweeper does its work, it emits fragrance into the room.

Don't neglect the basement or garage. Bunches of southernwood, mints, tansy and basil will freshen these areas.

And now for some recipes.

Most basic potpourri have roses as the principle bulk ingredient, so we will begin with one of these. The important thing in preparing dry potpourri is to have the flowers and herbs perfectly DRY—as crispy dry as breakfast cereal. Pick the roses, other flowers and herbs after the morning dew has evaporated and before the sun reaches its noonday heat. Spread the rose petals on several layers of newspaper and dry in an airy place. I dry my petals in the attic on an elevated screen and turn them every other day. They are usually dry in a week. Store in a brown paper bag until you have collected enough petals to make the potpourri. Dry some tiny rosebuds and leaves separately.

Dry some of your most fragrant herbs—the scented geraniums, thymes, rosemary, sweet marjoram, costmary, clove pinks, lavender, lemon verbena, bergamot, pineapple sage and a little mint. Dry each separately.

To give added color to the finished product, also dry some daisies, bachelor buttons, larkspur, calendula, bergamot blossoms, pansies and violets.

Stir the drying herbs occasionally and when they are perfectly dry, store in paper bags or opaque jars.

Certain roses will give that fragrance one associates with the old-fashioned potpourri which had its special place in grandmother's parlor. Especially fragrant are the very old roses such as *Rosa Damascena Bifera, Rosa Damascena Trigintipetala, Rosa Gallica Officinalis* and that old favorite, Cabbage Rose. The above roses may be purchased from Tillotson's Roses (address in back of book).

Of the later-day roses, I like Crimson Glory. Its fragrance, velvety red petals and many blossoms make its cultivation worthwhile.

When collecting ingredients for potpourri, don't overlook lemon, lime and orange peels. I save the peeling, scrape away the white inner skin and slice them into tiny slivers and dry to add citrus perfume to potpourri. Sometimes I stick cloves into larger sections of the peel, put this into the oven to dry and then grind this into a powder to add to sachets.

Before you get ready to combine the "treasures" you have been collecting, make sure you have some fixatives on hand. A fixative helps to blend the ingredients into a "oneness" and sets the fragrance. Fixatives also make the potpourri more lingering and give it a deeper note.

Some of the most used fixatives are orris root, calamus root, vetiver root, gum benzoin or tinctures such as musk, astro, civet and ambergris. These should be used sparingly. Naturally you will not need all of these. Some people are allergic to musk and orris root. I personally prefer ambergris, vetiver and gum benzoin. Combine the fixatives coarsely chopped and sliced with the spices.

Use a large container—a big crock, enameled roaster or kettle and stir the ingredients with a wooden spoon. Never use metal.

POTPOURRI WITH ROSE FRAGRANCE PREDOMINATING

> 8 cups rose petals including a few rosebuds and leaves
> 1 cup rose geranium leaves (Old Fashioned or
>   Attar preferred)
> 1 tablespoon of ground cloves
> 1 tablespoon allspice
> 2 tablespoons pieces gum benzoin
> 10 drops oil of roses

Mix thoroughly, put into a crock or opaque container and close tightly. Let set at least 6 weeks and stir or shake the mixture from time to time. The ingredients need this time to blend and to take away the rawness.

The following recipe is a sort of odds and ends of the flower garden—the kind of potpourri in which you can use a wide range of ingredients.

COUNTRY GARDEN POTPOURRI

> 8 cups dried rose petals
> 1 cup rose geranium leaves
> 1 cup Prince Rupert geranium (wonderful lemon fragrance)
> 1 cup lavender flowers and foliage
> 1 cup gillyflowers (clove pinks)
> 1 cup sweet woodruff

1 cup thyme
1 cup lemon vebena leaves
½ cup red bergamot flowers and leaves
¼ cup sweet marjoram
½ cup pineapple sage leaves
2 tablespoons gum benzoin
2 tablespoons orris root
2 tablespoons whole cloves
6 drops oil of heliotrope or other oil of one's choice
4 drops of vetiver oil

Mix together and age 6 weeks before putting into rose jars. The longer the ingredients blend, the more fragrant the potpourri will be. Add colorful flowers which you have dried such as larkspur, bachelor buttons, hyacinth florets, johnny jump-ups, sweet shrub, daisies (tiny English or wild daisies), fern and geranium florets.

Some potpourri recipes call for salt, a coarse salt being preferred. Pound a few bay leaves with the salt to incorporate more aroma. Potpourri made with salt tends to lose its color and should be used in an opaque container.

PERFUME TO SWEETEN LINEN

Mix in blender 1 ounce each of whole cloves, caraway seeds and allspice. Add 1 pound rose petals, ¼ pound bay salt. Mix thoroughly. May be put directly into bags.

Some of the old-time recipes gave measurements as handfuls. One copied from an old receipt book calls for:

four handfuls of fragrant rose petals
three handfuls of clove pinks
one handful rose geranium leaves
one handful of sweet marjoram

Place in layers, strewing fine salt thickly between each layer and mix well with an ounce of sliced orris root.

Another recipe lists two handfuls of lavender, two handfuls of rosemary, two of knotted sweet marjoram, two of lemon balm, two of pineapple sage, half a handful of orange or apple mint, some lemon and orange peel and ½ ounce of orris root. Chop or blend coarsely the following spices: 1 teaspoon each of whole cloves, cinnamon bark, sliced nutmeg. Mix with herbs. Store in a covered container and let age for 6 weeks.

Sachets are potpourri ingredients ground into powder with a few drops of fixative added. I use the electric blender for this job and it takes no time at all.

LEMON VERBENA

      2 cups dried lemon verbena leaves
      2 cups lemon balm
      2 cups Prince Rupert geranium leaves
Add ¼ cup orric powder, 2 cups cornstarch, some lemon peel, 6 drops oil of lemon and 6 drops oil of bergamot. Mix in blender and let age.

WOODSY SACHET

I use 4 ounces of orris root (can be diluted with cornstarch or rice flower), add 1 ounce lavender flowers, 1 ounce patchouli, handful rosemary, 1 teaspoon powdered cloves, 1 tablespoon pine needles, 1 tablespoon cedar. Sprinkle with 3 drops civet and 6 drops oak moss.

LAVENDER SACHET

Use 2 cups of the orris/cornstarch base and add 2 cups lavender flowers and 6 drops lavender oil.

SPICY SACHET

Mix in blender 2 cups dried rose petals, 2 cups marjoram, 1 cup cornstarch, ½ cup pineapple sage, ¼ cup powdered orris root, 2 bay leaves, 1 tablespoon each—caraway seed, allspice, cloves, nutmeg and cardamon seed.

One of the delights in using herbs you have raised and dried is the possibility of coming up with a special fragrance. Experiment!

I try (rather unsuccessfully) to keep a list and amount of what goes into the different batches of potpourri so if I really like the results it can be repeated.

Caswell-Massey in New York carries high grade ingredients for making potpourri. The address is listed in the back of the book.

DIRECTIONS FOR MAKING SMALL SACHETS

Patterns are given in this chapter for making up small sachets and include a boot, mitten, panty, Rosy and Granny Lavender "heads."

To make the heads, trace the faces onto flesh-colored material and paint in the features and hair with fabric dye. Cut out 2 circles for each head. With the right sides together, sew around the outside edge using a fine stitch. Leave a small opening at top of head for stuffing. Fill the head with some cotton liberally dusted with sachet powder. Sew closed.

The dust cap is cut from 2 circles which are sewn together around the outside edge. One circle has a small slit so the cap may be turned. Press edges and then sew a gathering stitch around the line marked in the pattern. Pull the threads to make the cap fit the head; it will completely cover the back of the head. Add a bit of cotton dusted with the sachet to the top of the cap and place on head, pulling the threads so that it fits. Thread a needle with some of the extra gathering thread and sew the cap here and there to the head. A ribbon may be added.

The panty sachet is made from sheer materials such as organdy, voile, dimity or silk with an overlay of matching net. A little design from lace cutouts and sequins may be sewn on before the net is added. Cut 2 layers of thin batting just a little bit smaller than the pattern. Put the sachet powder beween the layers and place between the organdy and net layers. Pin and sew a seam ¼ inch from the edge, using a fancy stitch. Pink the edges. Add a ribbon to the top to hide the seam.

The boot and mitten can be made from red felt with a white felt cuff or from red velvet using a fake fur cuff. Fill as in the other sachets. These are clever "tie-ons" for Christmas packages.

SACHETS

Leave Open At Top To Fill

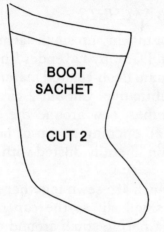

BOOT
SACHET

CUT 2

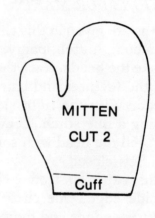

MITTEN

CUT 2

Cuff

Leave Open To Fill

Ribbon

PANTY

CUT 2

D.G.

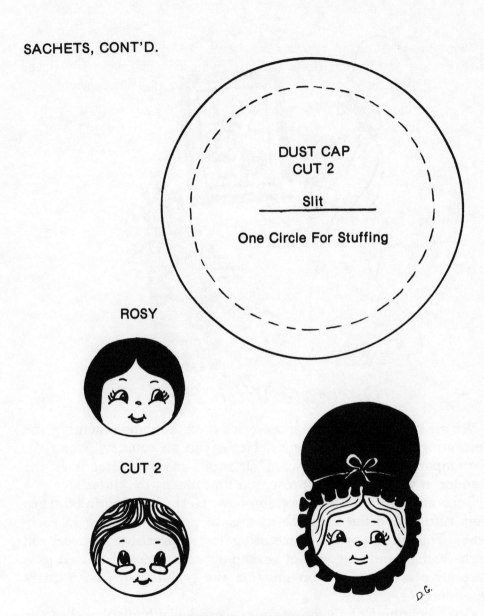

DUST CAP
CUT 2

Slit

One Circle For Stuffing

ROSY

CUT 2

GRANNY LAVENDER

*Patterns reduced 50%

Decorate With Herbs

We all know the impact accessories have in complementing the decorating theme in our homes. Herbs can go country, Victorian, contemporary, Early American, Oriental, modern, etc. It is the manner in which they are presented that makes the difference.

Decorating with herbs is nothing new. Herbs hanging in bunches from rafters and the fireplace mantel were commonplace in early times. Though this type of decorating had its practical purpose, the herbs being handy for instant seasoning, they were also used as a decorative accent. Can you imagine the pollution of those dusty seasonings?

Dried bouquets of Victorian times were lavishly displayed in the "busy" decor, however, many of them faded. Now, thanks to modern methods, the flowers and foliage retain most of their original color and form.

Pressed flower pictures have always been a delicate accent and collecting, pressing and identifying this flora was a favorite pastime for milady in the late '80's and early '90's.

Many of the herbal blossoms are dainty, but they have no equal for retaining true color. For example: red bergamot remains red; blue larkspur, blue; chives, mauve; lavender, purple; tansy button, golden; plate yarrow and pot marigolds stay bright yellow and orange.

The container sets the style for dried arrangements. For example: Oriental—okra pods and Japanese lanterns arranged in a low, black bowl; Modern—dried dock, cattails and yarrow used in a vertical arrangement in a terra cotta container; Victorian—dried rosebuds, baby's breath, lavender and bachelor buttons in a glass dome with a bird perched amidst the bouquet; a Williamsburg arrangement in milk glass.

Pictured in this chapter is a lavabo arrangement I have in my dining room. Though it is a very "full" arrangement, I am always finding space for a pretty red sassafras leaf, a sprig of sweet woodruff or a spike of lavender.

Hung on the dining room wall, the lavabo becomes a focal point for a wall arrangement. On either side of the lavabo is a decoupage plaque. One depicts "Common Remedies of Pilgrim Times," and the other, "Preparing Medicines From Herbs in Pilgrim Times." Over the plaques are dried pod pictures of contrived daisies (pumpkin seeds and teasel), lily pods and dock against a blue-green burlap background.

Directly below the lavabo is a glass-topped serving tray. The frame is antique blue-green and the background is blue and white checked gingham. The herbal bouquet is very colorful and uses chives, calendula, daisies, My Ladies Mantle, silvery wormwood, blue bachelor buttons, lavender, pink Love in a Mist, sweet woodruff and Queen Anne's Lace.

In three large oval Victorian frames with the convex glass domes, I use both pressed and natural form dried flowers. I use this arrangement over the living room sofa and pick up the colors of the room with a matting border and the flowers. The frames are becoming scarce today, but I am sure there are still some stashed away in attics. I don't know why, but I always feel sad when I remove the photograph which meant so much to someone long ago.

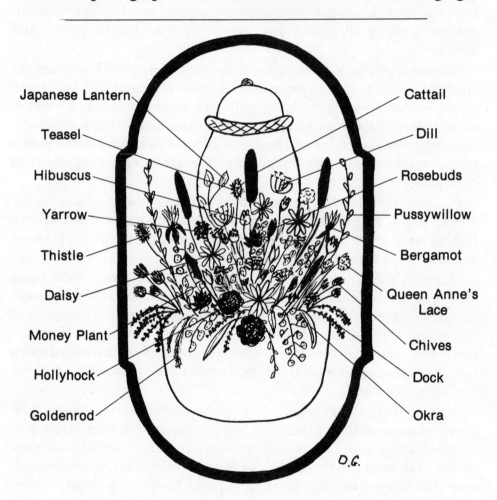

Japanese Lantern

Teasel

Hibuscus

Yarrow

Thistle

Daisy

Money Plant

Hollyhock

Goldenrod

Cattail

Dill

Rosebuds

Pussywillow

Bergamot

Queen Anne's Lace

Chives

Dock

Okra

D.G.

Dried Arrangement in Lavabo

Another way I have used pressed and dried herbs is on a three-way screen. The screen has 9 panel inserts and each insert features an old saying and the herb it describes. Like—"Basil Blesses All Food it Touches," with a spray of opal and green basil framing the saying. I used the screen once in a display when the late Euell Gibbons was speaking at one of his Wild Weekend appearances in our area. He and his wife, Freda, were both impressed and offered suggestions on how I could preserve it.

Perfect flower and foliage specimens individually framed in identical frames and hung in a group are effective accents. Pictures copied from old herbals or large pressed flower compositions identically framed and hung on a stairway wall are eye-catching.

Fresh herbs in pots and growing on a kitchen windowsill in hanging baskets and scented geraniums blooming in the tray of a dry sink can contribute to the popular live plant look.

Some other suggestions are: pressed herb designs used in glass paperweights; an herbal bouquet encased in a glass lamp base; matching spice jars brightly labeled and containing dried herbs on a spice rack; herb cookbooks on a kitchen shelf; a swag of dried herbs hanging from the mantel.

To press foliage and flowers, place between 4 sheets of newspaper and weight down. Change the paper the next day and the next if the herbs still feel moist. They take about a week to dry. You can "store" them between the pages of an old catalogue or between paper towels in a cardboard container.

One friend attributes her success in drying and pressing flowers to using 1 flower per book. She puts the flower between paper towels and between the middle pages of a book. Needless to say, she always has a pile of books stacked up. Another friend recommends drying the flowers and foliage between the pages of coloring books and weighting them down.

To dry flowers in silica gel, have an inch of the silica in the bottom of the container (preferably a cake or candy tin which seals tightly). Position the flower and carefully sift the medium over it until it is completely covered. If you plan to use the flower in a dried bouquet, wire it before putting in the gel. Keep the flowers separate; in other words, dry all zinnias or all roses at one time.

Other drying agents which work well with Queen Anne's Lace, zinnias and marigolds are cornmeal and borax. Keep the mixtures in a cardboard box. I like this method because the stems may be left on. This makes it easier to use them in arrangements. Put the flowers face down in several inches of the medium (enough to hold the stems straight). Brush off the medium after the flowers are dry and store them by inserting the stems into a block of styrafoam.

In the chapter on Tussie Mussies, we describe another decorative use for herbs, using them as accents in a 3-D arrangement. Herb stems, seed heads, etc., may be interwoven with yarn in wall hangings, in button gardens and seasonal door knockers.

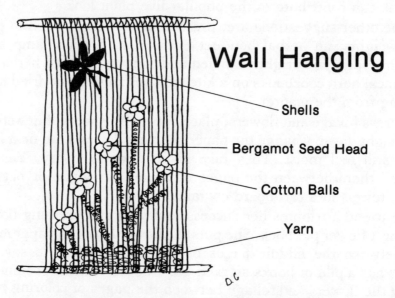

Wall Hanging

- Shells
- Bergamot Seed Head
- Cotton Balls
- Yarn

Herbs are becoming so popular nowadays that we find designs for afghans, crewel pictures and pillows, wallpaper, towels and curtains featuring herbs. There are many possibilities for decorating with herbs.

"And All Through The House"

Herbs blend beautifully with the aromas of Christmas and one can get a head start on the Christmas rush by making some of the decorations in the fall. I let my artemisia (Silver King) grow until late summer and make it into wreaths, swags and Christmas trees. I shape the decorations while the artemisia is fresh and pliable and put them away to dry in the attic until the holiday season.

To make a 3½-foot tree suitable for placing on a table, you will need at least 2 bushels of the fresh material. I prefer harvesting the artemisia while it is still ghostly white and before the brownish seed heads form.

First make a 4-foot cone from chicken wire. Fill the container with sand. Wooden planting tubs are fine. I use a little wooden bucket that salt fish was packed in and I have painted bright red. To secure the cone in the container, you may have to crush around the edges.

Sort the artemisia according to size, saving the long full branches to use at the bottom of the tree. Now begin at the top. Place a straight full branch for the top and start filling in around the cone. Keep the branches with the curves going upward. By the time you get to the bottom, you will be amazed at how the tree resembles a perfectly shaped blue spruce. Check for any bare spaces; the cone must be covered. Remember that the branches will shrink a little in the drying process. I always dry some extra artemisia to fill in with before starting to decorate the tree.

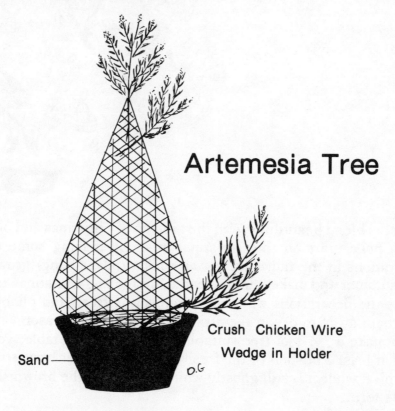

Artemesia Tree

Crush Chicken Wire
Wedge in Holder

Sand —

D.G

This type of tree needs the simplest decoration. I usually limit the trimming to two kinds, one of which is always colorful bows. Our favorite tree is decorated to please the grandchildren and for this I use little white felt mice carrying packages and wreaths or playing tiny musical instruments.

Use the pattern given for the pennyroyal mouse. The boots and hat for the male mice are made from red felt, the dress and dust cap for the female mice are made out of red flannel. They can be placed among the branches with only their chenille tails to hold them in position. The bows are made from red and white polka dot ribbon.

Other decorating themes could be little birds' nests made from dried grasses and sprayed a soft green or mustard yellow. Colorful birds in the nest add the finishing touch.

Another choice is the little replicas of market baskets available at craft shops. Spray paint the baskets one color and fill with potpourri which you have gathered into little net squares secured with a rubber band.

Artemisia wreaths can also be made ahead of time. I use a wire wreath frame and wire small bunches of the material to the base. Have the material going in the same direction. Once the wreath is covered, you can fill in with shorter pieces of the artemisia until the wreath is nice and fat. Hang it up to dry so that it will keep the roundness. I use double bows on these—one to show from the outside and one from the inside, otherwise they are perfectly plain.

For a more decorative wreath to use in the hallway or over the fireplace, add herbs that blend with the decor. These will be decorated on one side. Use little clusters of tiny rosebuds for a lacy Victorian wreath (I dry the buds from an old-fashioned pink rambler). Before putting them in a drying medium, I push a thin wire through the little knob at the bud's base, so all I need to do when trimming is gather the wires together to make bunches of the buds. These are attached to the wreath by securing to the wire frame. Sprays of fragrant lavender dried by the hanging method are pushed into the base. Add baby's breath and a bow to fill in and give an airy look.

A wreath symbolizing the religious signifigance of Christmas can be made with Biblical herbs. Use the same type base of artemisia and add sprigs of rosemary. This herb, legend tells us, was kind to the Holy family when they were fleeing Egypt. The other trees and bushes rustled and made much noise, but the rosemary kept silent. When Mary threw her blue mantle over the rosemary's white blossoms to dry, the blossoms turned blue. The bitter herbs of passover, such as wormwood, horehound and rue, can be fashioned into little clusters and wired on picks, then inserted into the wreath. The dried mauve blossoms of mint (one of the tithing herbs), thyme (the manger herb), and pennyroyal and costmary (Bible leaf) can be used alternately for the inside center of the wreath. Add a bow and attach little net bags holding frankincense, myrrh, a stick of cinnamon and whole cloves.

Artemesia Wreath

Keep Foliage Going in Same Direction

A wreath made up for the kitchen will feature culinary herb leaves and seeds. This wreath I also make in the fall so the herbs will not shatter. Using an artemisia base, wire together bunches of savory (winter), seed head sprigs of sweet basil, sprigs of thyme, dill umbels, feathery fennel, mauve blossoms of wild marjoram, clusters of sage and chive blossoms. (Some of the herbs, such as chives were dried earlier by the ''upside-down'' method). A big blue and white gingham bow is the finishing touch.

For the big, fresh pine tree, I use herbal ornaments in shades of turquoise and pale blue. The Victorian shoes are fashioned of turquoise nylon velvet with matching and contrasting trims. Some are left-handed and others right-handed. These are filled with a stuffing of plastic dry-cleaning bags and enough lavender blossoms to give a strong fragrance. Little market baskets painted a soft shade of blue hold net-filled potpourri of different fragrances. They make a remembrance gift to give to guests.

Victorian dolls dressed in turquoise velvet wear fur-trimmed bonnets and muffs filled with sachet. The faces are hand-painted on flesh-colored cotton which has been glued to thin cardboard.

Spices such as cinnamon sticks, nutmegs and whole cloves are gathered into nylon net bags and tied to the branches with a bow. Pomanders are hung on the sturdier branches.

Making the pomanders several weeks before Christmas is traditional at our house. The fragrance of the oranges curing in spices gives a getting-ready-for-Christmas air before the pine tree comes on the scene.

Pomander comes from the French word *pomme*, meaning apple. Originally made to mask unpleasant odors and to ward off plagues, doctors carried walking sticks which had little compartments to hold aromatic herbs. One may use apples, lemons or oranges for a base. I prefer oranges because they always turn out right. Try to find oranges without too thick a skin so that the cloves will be easier to push into the orange. Sometimes it is necessary to make a small hole with a nut pick in order to insert the clove. Make rows of cloves close together and be sure to finish the pomander at one sitting (the fruit will shrink). Sometimes I rub the orange with a piece of cotton dampened with a fixative (musk astro or civet), but this is not necessary. When the orange is completely studded with cloves, it will be rolled in a curing medium. This is made up with equal parts of powdered orris root and ground cinnamon. A few drops of bergamot or orange oil may be added. Be sure that the fruit is well-dusted with the mixture. You can put them in a bowl and allow to dry at room temperature or you can wrap each orange in tissue paper; store for a week to ripen. Wrap a cord around the fruit if you wish to hang them on the tree and in a clothes closet.

To tie in with our Victorian theme, we made a huge shoe copying the one we use on the tree. Filled with stuffing and potpourri, it adds glamour to the fireplace decorations.

While visiting a novelty shop in Innsburg, Austria, we saw Christmas ornaments made out of black walnuts. Seeds in geometrical designs were glued to the shell.

MAKING PENNYROYAL AND CATNIP MICE

The pennyroyal mice are made from lightweight grey felt and stuffed with a mixture of polyester cotton and pennyroyal. A grey chenille wire is used for the tail.

To make the colorful white felt mice for the artemisic tree, use thin weight felt. Patterns for the cap, boots and dust cap and dress are given here. The dress and dust cap for the female mice are made with red flannel. Use the pattern lines of the mouse for the seam lines, and make the stitch very tight as they will fray easily. No matter how carefully I cut them out and sew them, they always come out different sized, which I guess is just as well. A variety is better.

PENNYROYAL MOUSE

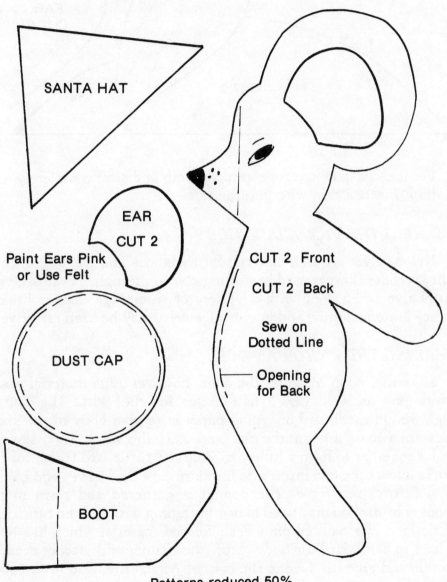

SANTA HAT

EAR
CUT 2

Paint Ears Pink
or Use Felt

CUT 2 Front

CUT 2 Back

Sew on
Dotted Line

DUST CAP

Opening
for Back

BOOT

Patterns reduced 50%

Catnip Mouse

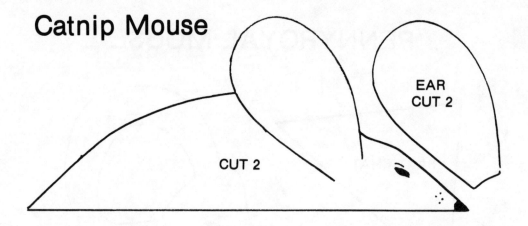

EAR
CUT 2

CUT 2

For the catnip mouse, use a sturdy cloth and stuff completely with catnip. Insert a thin wire into the tail.

MAKING THE VICTORIAN SHOES

Nylon velvet is a rich material for the shoes and the fragrance of the lavender flowers used in stuffing comes through. These are very attractive when done with a variety of trimmings. Laces, braids, fancy buttons, leftover oddments of jewelry may be used effectively.

MAKING THE VICTORIAN DOLL

I also use nylon velvet for the dolls, however other material would work just as well. Cut 2 half-circles for the skirt. The one of lightweight cardboard or typing paper is to give body to the skirt. Sew the two together at the hem and down the sides. Then sew the sides together to form a full skirt. Fold the cardboard frame for the torso into a cone and insert into the skirt. Sew the sleeves and blouse and fit over the torso. The bonnet is gathered and sewn to the bonnet brim. You may need to use stiffening between the brim. The little faces are painted onto flesh-colored material which has been glued to cardboard for body. Stuff the bonnet with sachet-scented cotton and glue the face to the cotton. Attach the head to the body

VICTORIAN
VELVET SHOE

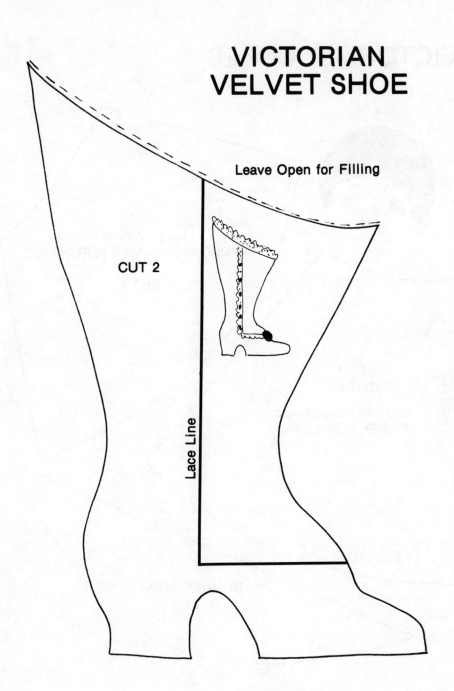

Leave Open for Filling

CUT 2

Lace Line

VICTORIAN DOLLS

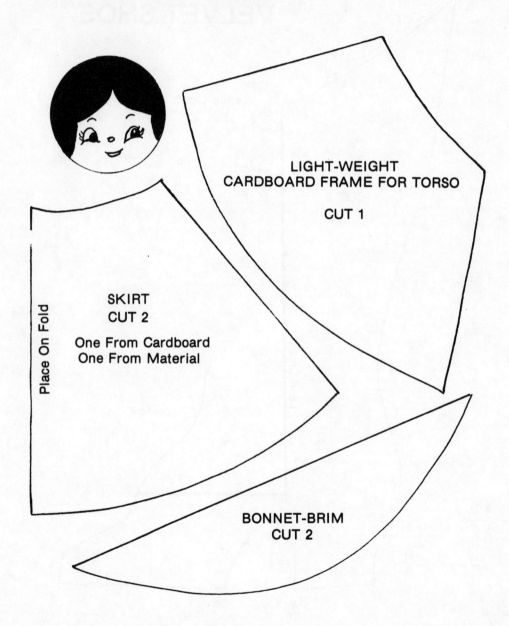

LIGHT-WEIGHT
CARDBOARD FRAME FOR TORSO

CUT 1

Place On Fold

SKIRT
CUT 2

One From Cardboard
One From Material

BONNET-BRIM
CUT 2

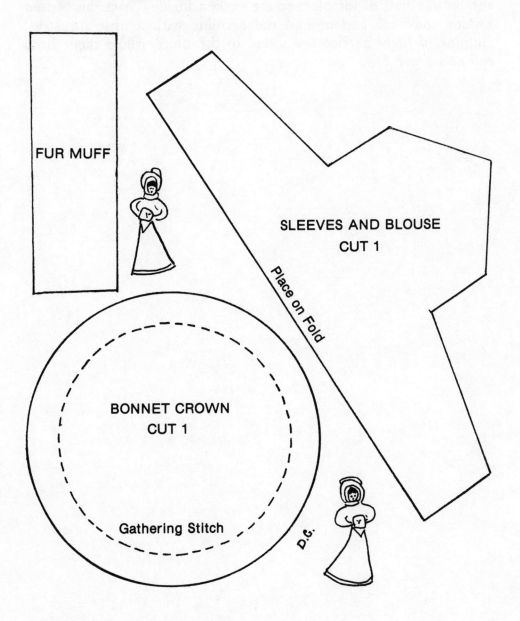

FUR MUFF

SLEEVES AND BLOUSE
CUT 1

Place on Fold

BONNET CROWN
CUT 1

Gathering Stitch

D.G.

with a big corsage pin. The muff is made from white fur material and the bottom half of the sleeves are tucked inside. Trim the bonnet around the neck and around the hemline with a little fur strip. Cutouts of holly berries are glued to the muff. Make them from red and green felt.

Say It
With A Tussie Mussie

Taking a tussie mussie to one's hostess was a thoughtful gesture in mid-Victorian times—a fragrant way of saying "thank you." The little nosegays were even more effective in the "courting game." They carried a message—sometimes good and sometimes not so good— depending on the disposition of the giver.

The miniature bouquets, which could be held in the hand, were centered with the flower carrying the main message. Surrounding this center flower, dainty foliage and blossoms gave contributing thoughts.

For an example, a tussie mussie centered with an angelica umbel said: "You are my inspiration." If it was surrounded with coriander, it elaborated with "you have hidden worth." The object of these declarations would send back her reply. If she were interested, it could be a China aster, meaning "I will think on it;"if she could care less, an ice plant went back telling him "to forget it."

A few of the flower meanings are listed below and one can readily see that keeping a "Flora Dictionary" handy was almost a necessity.

Some meanings were self-explanatory: Borage with its dainty blue star-shape flowers meant courage; Lily signified purity;

Sage—immortality; White Violet—innocence; Rosemary—remembrance; Red Rose—love; Rue—repentence; Mint—wisdom; Mugwort—weary traveler; Pennyroyal—flee away and Poppy—oblivion.

Herbs joined with familiar flowers in conveying practically every thought and emotion a would-be lover wanted to express. Buglass meant falsehood; Burnet suggested a happy heart; Camomile—patience; Chicory—frugality; Dandelion—oracle; Elder—compassion; Fennel—flattery; Forget-me-not symbolized true love; Foxglove—adulation; Fumitory—hatred; Hollyhock—ambition; Horehound—health; Hyssop—sacrifice; Larkspur—fickleness; Laurel—glory; Lavender—mistrust; Lily-of-the-Valley signified return to happiness; Pansy—sad thoughts; Marjoram—happiness; Marigold—grief; Parsley—festivity; Nasturtium—patriotism; Pimpernal—assignation; Clove Pink—resignation; Yellow Rose—infidelity; Musk Rose—capricious beauty; Saffron—mirth; Sorrell—parental affection: Southernwood—constancy; Speedwell-fidelity; Stonecrop—tranquility; Sunflower—false riches; Tansy—hostile thoughts; Thrift—sympathy; Thyme—bravery; Valerian—readiness; Verbena—delicacy of feeling; Blue Violet—loyalty; Basil—either love or hate; Wormwood—displeasure.

The first tussie mussie I ever saw was back in the early '40's when one of our sons was in the hospital recuperating from an eye operation. My next door neighbor brought over a fragrant little bouquet and said: "I know Terry's eyes are bandaged and he won't be able to see the flowers but I think he will enjoy the fragrance." I closed my eyes and the fragrance was intensified. In the bouquet were tiny rosebuds, clove pinks, rose geranium leaves, orange mint, some dainty thyme blossoms, a sprig of lemon verbena and a sprig of pineapple sage. Since that time I have tried to keep little herb sachets made up to be enclosed with get-well cards, especially to those in the hospital.

The time to make up tussie mussies is when flowers are in season. Tussie mussies are quite simple to make and ingenuity is limited only by the flowers on hand and your imagination. Most every gardener grows roses, so let's start out with a single rose. Cut the stem at least 3 inches long. The rose will be the center. Encircle the rose with baby's breath, statice, sweet alyssum, or thyme blossoms. Be sure to keep the stems long. Next, add a row of bachelor buttons or wild daisies. The last circle should be greenery for contrast. This could be any of the mints, ferns, scented geranium leaves or rosemary sprigs. Wrap a thin wire around the stems and put into a glass of water and store overnight in the refrigerator. This hardens the flowers and keeps them fresh longer.

When you are ready to add the finishing touches, wrap the upper part of the stem in floral tape and the lower half with cotton or a paper towel which has been dampened. Protect this covering with foil. Push the stems through a paper doily and attach a narrow ribbon bow and streamers. The tussie mussie is ready to be put in a glass of water when it arrives at its destination.

Since paper doilies often become wet and limp, I make up my own basic collars for the nosegays. Cut a circle 3 inches in diameter from a plastic lid (like lids used on coffee). Cut out the center, leaving an inch rim. Cut a cone 3 inches long from the plastic and fasten the ends with a few stitches. Now insert the cone thourgh the circle. It should fit tight. Make a 2-inch ruffle from nylon net and sew this to the top of the circle. You now have a waterproof form. Nylon lace forms may be purchased at the florists.

The tussie mussie is one of the most creative bouquets you can make and the fragrant herbs with their dainty foliage and blossoms add to its beauty. Imagine blue or white violets, clove pinks and coral bells together; lavender flowers with pink valerian blossoms and a border of pineapple sage; an-oh-so-fragrant moss rose encircled with baby's-breath and lavender spikes, or sprigs of lilac encircled with lily-of-the-valley!

Tussie mussies may also be fashioned with dried materials. One of my favorite wall hangings is a large picture frame backed with blue gingham and a sheet of music. On the right hangs my violin and in the left-hand corner a lacy tussie mussie of wild daisies, blue bachelor buttons and tansy fern.

In keeping with the earth tones used in decoration, a tussie mussie made of yellow and orange strawflowers, encircled with brown dock and tan wheat in a doily of a contrasting shade could be mounted on a burlap or small cotton print background and framed.

An easy way to assemble a dried tussie mussie is to use a small styrofoam cone. Strawflowers must be wired by bringing a wire with a hook on one end down the center of the flower. Dock and wheat have firm stems and will not need to be wired. Insert the strawflowers in the center of the cone and circle alternately with dock and wheat. Push through the ready-made form and add ribbon and streamers. Spray the completed bouquet with a fixative (hair lacquer will do).

The tussie mussie just described is not fragrant, however there are some herbs which may be used that are: the seed head of bergamot; lavender sprays; sweet woodruff (which has the odor of new mown hay after it drys). Yellow tansy buttons, powderpuff hollyhocks, santolina, the yarrows, and My Lady's Mantle, are also good choices.

Tussie mussies to add glamour to a Christmas package can be made from dill seeds, Queen Anne's Lace and a collar of net. Dry the umbels when they are at the green stage (the seeds will not fall out) and spray with flat white floral paint. While still wet, sprinkle on diamond dust.

For Christmas color, tint Queen Anne's Lace by inserting the stem into water in which food coloring has been dissolved. Use as center of nosegay. Spray with lacquer and sprinkle on matching glitter for extra sparkle. Attach to package with a corsage pin.

Or, why not make a corsage for the men in your life (this one is not feminine)! Use a small circle or square of stryofoam the size of a silver dollar. Insert 2-inch cuttings of fresh herb foliage such as sage, santolina, rue, winter savory, lamb's ear, sweet basil, lavender spikes, thyme and tansy blossoms. Tie a tiny ribbon bow and fasten with wire to complete. These may also be placed in closets and used as moth repellents.

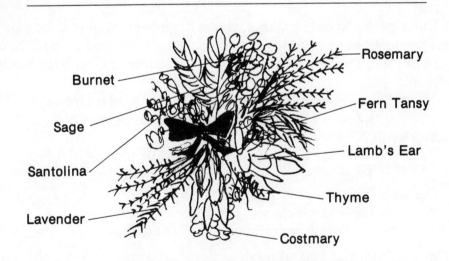

Burnet

Sage

Santolina

Lavender

Rosemary

Fern Tansy

Lamb's Ear

Thyme

Costmary

Package Corsage

Make Life Beautiful For Felix And Fido

What better way to make life beautiful for one's cat and dog than to keep them healthy and comfortable. Here again, we can look to herbs!

Those pesky trouble-makers, fleas, have been around a long time and people have been trying out ways for centuries to be rid of them. Back in 1580, Tusser in his *Five Hundred Points of Good Husbandry* advised:

> "Where chamber is swept, and Wormwood is strown,
>   No Flea for his life dare abide to be known."

And again:

> "What savour is better, if physic be true,
>   For places infected, than Wormwood Rue."

The *Schola Salernitana* had this to say:

> "Rue maketh chaste; and it preserveth the sight;
>   Infuseth wit, and putteth fleas to flight."

Wormwood and rue, though super repellents, are not the only herbs that befriend pets. Camomile blossoms (some recommend frying the flowers and scattering them around), the mints, tansy and pennyroyal are all effective in keeping dogs and cats more comfortable.

Oil of pennyroyal (a very small amount goes a long way) added to olive oil or glycerin and gently massaged through the animal's fur will rid the pet of fleas.

Pennyroyal oil is often rubbed on horses to repel stinging flies. A weak tea of pennyroyal sprayed over the roosts and the poultry will cleanse them from lice.

I make little grey felt mice and stuff them with pennyroyal. They are fastened to the pet's sleeping basket by their chenille tails.

Make a pillow of ticking or some other sturdy fabric to fit the pet's bed. Stuff the pillow with a little polyester and a combination of the following herbs—tansy, mint, smaller amounts of pennyroyal, rue and camomile. If you do not grow all of these herbs, a combination of two or more will be effective.

If cats are your passion, be sure and keep a supply of catnip around. Gerard says: "The later herbalists do call it 'Herba Cattanin' because the cats are very much delighted herewith, for the smell of it is so pleasant to them that they rub themselves upon it, and wallow or tumble in it, and also feed on the branches and leaves very greedily."

An old rime says:

"If you set it, the catts will eate it,
If you sow it, the catts won't know it."

And this rime is certainly true. Once cats get a whiff of the herb, they will really tear up the garden getting to it. I try to sow it in an out-of-the-way spot that doesn't invite feline traffic.

Catnip is always a good seller at fairs and bazaars as it seems few people do grow it. I like to make up little grey felt mice and stuff them with the herb and give them to friends who own cats. Patterns for the pennyroyal mouse and the catnip mouse can be found on page 76.

Just mention an herb and you will discover a legend. The following relates to puppies.

According to the doctrine of signatures, the English Daisy, a diminutive plant with roots to correspond, was once thought to arrest the bodily growth. The roots were boiled in broth and given to young puppies to keep them of small size.

If the dog or cat is ''off its food'' and tired of regular fare, try adding a touch of minced garlic to the food. It will become more appetizing to the pet.

Herbs Help
The Gardener

"The Lord hath created medicines out of the earth; and he that is wise will not abhor them."

—*Ecclesiasticus 37, verse 4*

Herbalists have found this scripture to be true, even when planting a garden, for the Lord has provided plants to nurture other plants and plants which repel destroying insects. We must, however, keep the laws of nature balanced. The gardener can do his or her part by observing some of these natural aids.

For safer, healthier and easier gardening, give herbs a chance. You'll find much "virtue" in companion planting, odiferous herbs, herb mulches, powders and sprays—nature's way.

Every spring we encircle our vegetable garden plot with marigolds. Most of the time my husband manages to plow some of them out as he goes back and forth between the rows of plants, which means a big transplanting job for me, but the dividends far outweigh the labor. We use a variety—French marigolds, the big orange and yellow and mum marigolds. I always have a row of pot marigold growing in the garden for culinary purposes. I am always happy to see the marigolds come up as they divert the rabbits from my scented geraniums. The little fellows will sit up and nibble on the marigold foliage, but they will eat my poor geraniums completely to the ground. Just as a precaution, I place wire cages around the geraniums.

Wormwood planted along the garden fence will discourage stray animals from venturing into the garden. However, be careful where you plant the wormwood as it leeches and is harmful to some plants.

Tansy, both the fern and button top varieties, are attractive plants and perhaps the most versatile plant for repelling insect pests. Planted near peach trees, it repels borers and, near the grape vines, it discourages Japanese beetles. It deters flies and ants, and sprinkled in the cupboards will get rid of the latter pests.

Camomile is known as the plant physician—planted near an ailing plant it will revive it and make it healthy again. Plant with cabbage and onions.

It has been proven that companion planting gives the best results in production for the gardener. Plants, like people, have aversions, and in cases like this, avoidance is the answer. Rue, for example, will deter Japanese beetles but should not be planted near sweet basil. Dill should be planted with cabbage but never with carrots.

I like to have several basil plants by the kitchen door as they repel flies, and, if one believes in the Hindu superstition, they also protect the household from evil. Why take a chance? Basil quite naturally is a good companion to tomatoes.

Borage is also a good companion to tomatoes as it deters tomato worms. It is also helpful when planted with strawberries. Catnip repels flea beetles and can be planted in borders.

Good radishes are rare unless precautions are taken. Chervil planted next to radishes seems to help. Chives should be planted next to carrots; flax between rows of potatoes. Horseradish also repels the potato bug.

Cabbage needs all the help it can get to stay free from moths. A few hyssop plants, mint, and nasturtium all repel the cabbage moth.

Hyssop is also helpful planted near grapes, and nasturtiums near fruit trees, and as a companion to cabbage and cucumbers. It deters aphids and squash bugs. Rosemary is still another companion plant for cabbage. It also deters bean beetles and is a good companion to sage, beans and carrots. Summer savory, the bean herb, combats bean beetles.

Some herbs are good planted in borders or at random in the garden. These include sweet marjoram, lovage, bee balm, and mint. Because I reserve one bed of roses exclusively for culinary purposes, I must depend on herbs to keep them healthy. A border of chives is planted with roses along with santolina, some garlic buds, fern tansy and lavender.

Capitalize on the herbs as mulches. When weeding out the mints—and they are certainly prolific—strip the leaves from the stalks and use as a mulch. Also use the remnants from herbal teas. Our comfrey always gets ahead of us and whenever we cut the plant back, we snip up some of the leaves for a mulch and add the heavier stalks to the compost pile.

Herb sprays are often needed to fight off some of the pests. A blender comes in handy for this job. To make a garlic or chive spray, put the herb into the blender with water. Strain the resulting purée through cheese cloth, add a little detergent to make the spray stick to the plant. Put into hand sprayer and use on infested plants.

A strong tea made from tansy, wormwood and mint is another effective spray.

Dried herbs such as pyrethrum (used today in a number of commercial insecticides), feverfew, wormwood, stinging nettle, tansy, rue, southernwood and rosemary can be reduced to a powder and then dusted on and around plants. This will help keep ants away.

The worst intruders in our garden are moles—and now, maybe an herb will be taking care of this problem. I'm planting *Euphorbia Lathyris* or Moleplant. The use of this plant, planted near the beds, is said to be helpful in preventing mole intrusions.

Now I Lay Me Down To Sleep. . .I Hope!

Many herbs are listed as sophorics. Two of the most common are lettuce and dill. Pope said: "For want of rest, lettuce and cowslip wine, probatum est."

"Dill," which comes from the Norse word *dilla* meaning "to lull," was made into a warm tea and given to babies to make them sleep. Dill was also one of the "meeting" seeds given to children to chew on during a long church service to keep them quiet.

Sophoric sponges, actually a sort of herbal anaesthesia, were used in Ancient China and contained henbane as one of the ingredients. Some of the early recipes for pomanders contained herbs that induced sleep—herbs such as hemlock, mandrake and opium poppy. We hasten to add that one will never find these growing in our garden.

Perhaps our readers will recall the onion tea our grandmothers would brew to cure a cold. It was a reliable standby. Raw onions or Spanish onions which have been stewed and then eaten before retiring was another oldtime way to guarantee a good sleep. Culpepper, however, says this does not apply to chives: "If eaten raw," he warns, "they send up very hurtful vapours to the brain, causing troublesome sleep and spoiling the eyesight." That's warning enough for me!

According to her publicity department, Mae West (who seems to defy the ravages of aging) eats a raw onion sandwich every night upon retiring.

We discussed herbal teas in an earlier chapter, but we must include some of the teas which are helpful in lulling one to sleep. Three highly recommended are camomile, anise and southernwood. Anise tea is made by bruising ¼ teaspoon of the seeds. Simmer them in 1 cup of milk and drink while it is still warm upon retiring.

John Hill wrote his recipe for Southernwood Tea in his *The British Herbalist* (1772). It goes as follows:

"Clip 4 ounces of the leaves fine and beat them in a mortar with 6 ounces of loaf sugar till the whole is like a paste. Three times a day take the bignesse of a nutmeg of this. It is pleasant and one thing in particular, it is a composer and always disposes persons to sleep."

New Jersey Tea (*Ceanothus americanus*), a popular tea during the Revolutionary War, is a mild sedative.

Slumber pillows were commonplace and many recipes are included in the old herbals. One such recipe still in use today is from *Ram's Little Dodoen* (1606), and was described as "A Bag To Smell Into For Melancholy, Or To Cause One to Sleep—Take drie Rose leaves, keep them close in a glasse which will keep them sweet, then take powder of Mints, powder of Cloves in a grosse powder and put the same to the Rose leaves, then put all these together in a bag, and take that to bed with you and it will cause you to sleep, and it is good to smell into at other times."

Translated into everyday language, here is our version: Put into an electric blender 2 cups dried rose petals, 2 cups mint leaves (orange, lavender, spearmint or stone mint), ½ ounce of ground cloves and ½ ounce of powdered orris root. Make little pillows 6 by 9 inches from a soft material. Put the ground mixture between 2 thin layers of polyester filling and sew closed.

Hops (*Humulus lupulus*) have been popular herbs for filling pillows to induce slumber. The hops should be sprinkled with alcohol to soften them. Royalty was not adverse to trying out these simple slumber helpers—King George III slept on a pillow filled with hops.

Rosemary with its fresh pine fragrance, lemon balm, lemon grass, lemon verbena, Prince Rupert and the rose geraniums, and, of course, lavender, are all good herbs to use for slumber pillows. Combine the above and add a fixative such as gum benzoin for a more lasting fragrance.

It was William Turner who wrote: "I judge that the flowers of lavender quilted in a cap and dayly worne are good for all diseases of the head and that they comfort the braine very well."

Following Turner's suggestion, I've designed some sleep pillows and "nite-nite" dolls with lavender or a potpourri sewn into the dust cap.

Today's toddlers seem dependent on their security blankets. Just try to take one away from the child to launder and you'll have a battle on your hands. The three cuddly dolls are offered as a substitute. Granny Lavender, Rosy and Herby are partially filled with herbs so the fragrance will be released when the child hugs them.

To make the Granny and Rosy Pillow you will need flesh-colored cotton or unbleached muslin. Cut two from the pattern and paint on the features with acrylics, fabric paint or embroider. Partially fill with polyester filling and pour the potpourri mixture into the center. Have the cotton filling next to the face side for a smoother appearance. The dust cap is a large circle 14 inches in diameter (I find a wooden serving tray is just the right size for the pattern). Sew the circle completely around the edges with the right sides together, then cut a 3-inch slit in one of the circles and turn. Press down the outside edge and sew on lace if desired. Now make a double row of gathering stitches 1½ inches from outside edge. Pull threads to make ruffle. Place some of the rose potpourri in Rosy's dust cap and sew up slit. Add a little of the cotton filling to make the cap tall and full. Take some fringe or make yarn hair to cover area marked on patterns. Bring the dust cap down across the back so the ruffle is at the base of the head. Sew lightly to the head and cover the stitches with a ribbon. Granny Lavender's dust cap is made from a pretty lavender cotton and is filled with lavender flowers. Rosy's dust cap is made from rose-red cotton. A rose-flower print would be attractive. Of course, the caps can be made any color to match the decor.

SLUMBER PILLOWS

Granny Lavender

Rosy

For the Dust Cap, cut circle 14'' in diameter. Sew outside edges completely. Slit 1 circle in center. Turn and sew 2 rows of gathering stitch ½'' from the outside edge to make ruffles. Leave 2½'' for opening in back; cut ½'' band for stand-up collar. Cut 2'' strip 3 times the size of the Hemline for ruffles.

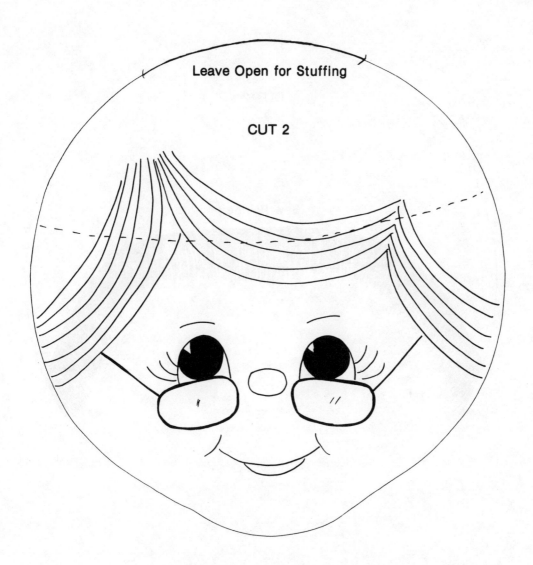

Leave Open for Stuffing

CUT 2

Granny Slumber Pillow

*Patterns reduced 50%

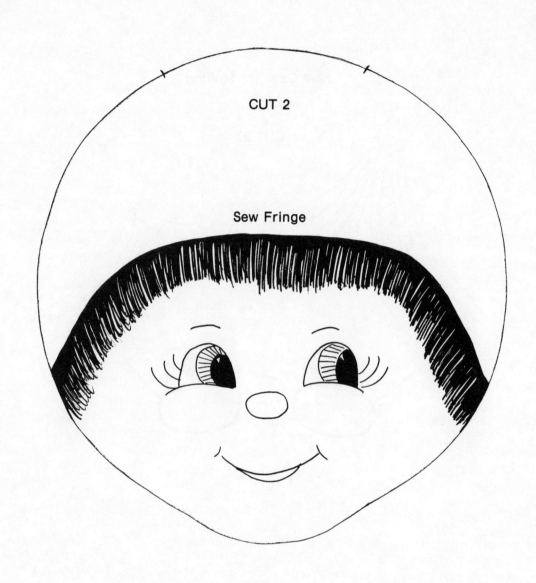

CUT 2

Sew Fringe

Rosy Slumber Pillow

MAKING THE HERB DOLLS

A basic body pattern can be used for all three dolls. However, Herby does have a different head. It is sewn on flush with the neck, which must be turned down 1 inch. The features are painted on with fabric dye or acrylic paints. Fringe may be used for Rosy's hair. Yarn or the regular wig fabric may be cut to fit Granny and Herby.

ROSY   GRANNY LAVENDER   HERBY

Trace Granny's and Rosy's head on wrong side of fabric and use the lines as a stitching guide. Put right sides together and stitch the pieces together, leaving an opening at the top of the head for stuffing. Carefully trim around the chin and cheeks. Turn. Stuff head tightly. Whip stitch neck to back of head, about ¾'' along top sides of neck and across top of neck. This will be covered with hair later. Insert a popsicle stick or tongue depressor in neck and stuff body. Use plenty of stuffing and pour in a cup full of the herb you are using for scent. By attaching the head this way, you will have a chin line.

Cut out the body, allowing ¼-inch seams. Use flesh-colored cotton or unbleached muslin. Leave open at neck to stuff (as the pillows were filled). Sew the arms and the legs on the seam line as shown, then cut out. The nose is gathered and stuffed with cotton and put on the faces with small stitches.

A soft polyester knit is a nice choice for Herby's pajamas. I use a soft green and paint his eyes the same shade of green. The pattern is marked with directions. Use a lot of herbal filling in Herby, since he doesn't have the dust cap to fill.

Rosy's dress and cap are rose-red cotton and her panties are a rose-flowered print. I use black fringe for her hair and paint her eyes black. Put the cap on the head as in the pillow, letting the back of the cap completely cover the back of the head.

Granny is dressed in lavender or purple and her dress is a little fancier with matching lace trim around the panties, around the neck, the cuffs and the dust cap.

Add a little extra length to the dress for Rosy and Granny. Allow the ruffles to come to the edge of the hemline.

Bigger dolls may be made by ''blowing up'' the patterns. A bag of polyester filling will be enough to stuff all three. A yard of muslin will be enough to make three bodies. It takes ¾ yard of cotton for one dust cap and dress. Make the cap just like the one on the pillow doll, but reduce the diameter to 13 inches.

HERB DOLL PATTERNS

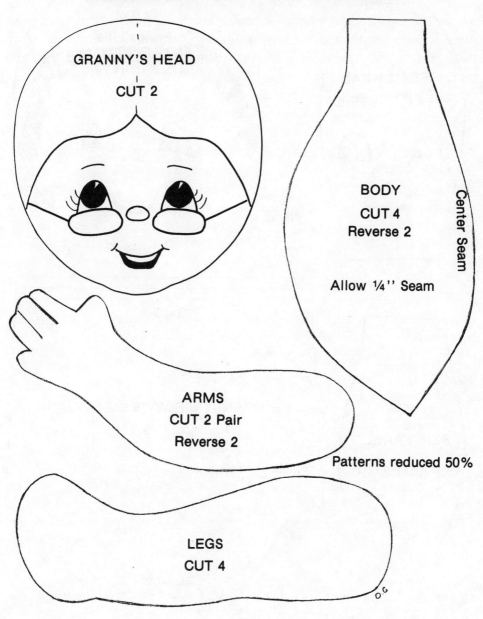

GRANNY'S HEAD

CUT 2

BODY

CUT 4
Reverse 2

Allow ¼'' Seam

Center Seam

ARMS

CUT 2 Pair

Reverse 2

Patterns reduced 50%

LEGS

CUT 4

O.G.

103

HERB DOLL PATTERNS, CONT'D.

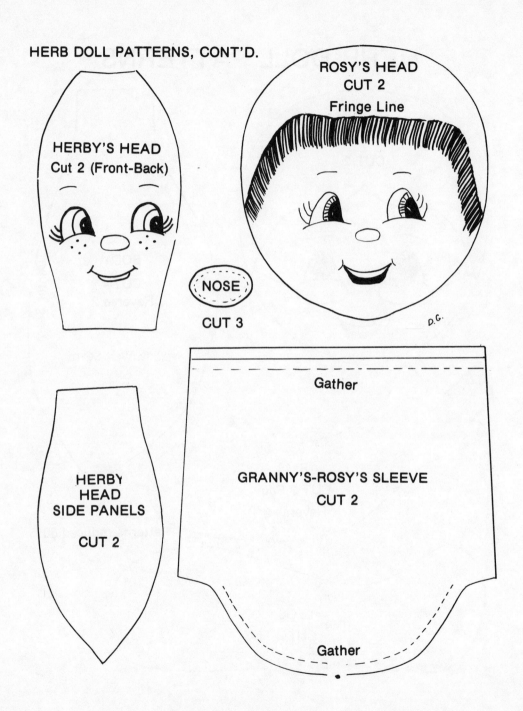

HERBY'S HEAD
Cut 2 (Front-Back)

ROSY'S HEAD
CUT 2
Fringe Line

NOSE
CUT 3

D.G.

HERBY HEAD SIDE PANELS
CUT 2

Gather

GRANNY'S-ROSY'S SLEEVE
CUT 2

Gather

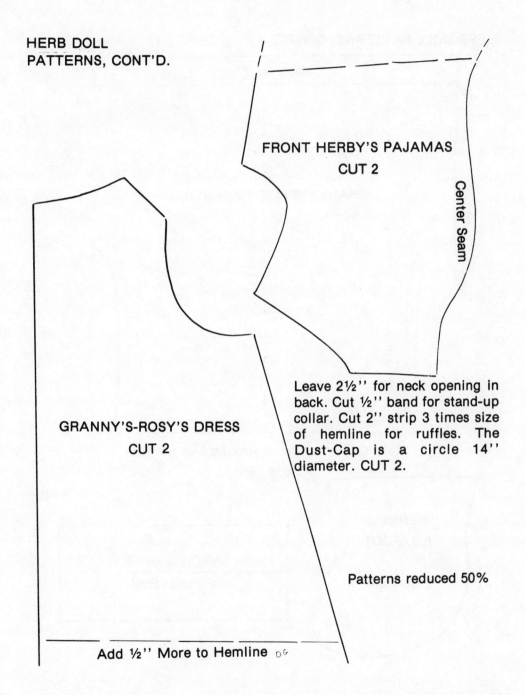

FRONT HERBY'S PAJAMAS
CUT 2

Center Seam

GRANNY'S-ROSY'S DRESS
CUT 2

Leave 2½'' for neck opening in back. Cut ½'' band for stand-up collar. Cut 2'' strip 3 times size of hemline for ruffles. The Dust-Cap is a circle 14'' diameter. CUT 2.

Patterns reduced 50%

Add ½'' More to Hemline DG

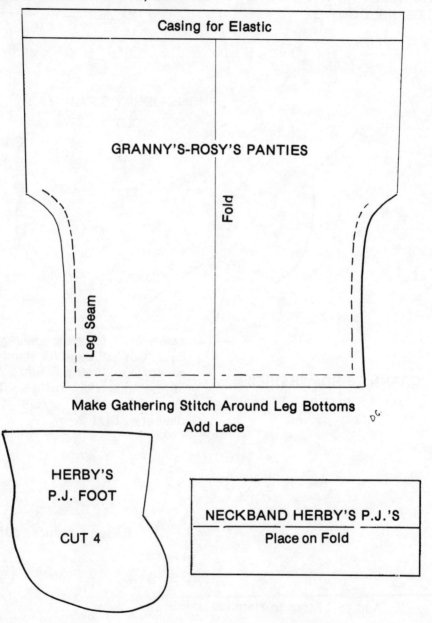

Casing for Elastic

GRANNY'S-ROSY'S PANTIES

Fold

Leg Seam

Make Gathering Stitch Around Leg Bottoms

Add Lace

DC.

HERBY'S
P.J. FOOT

CUT 4

NECKBAND HERBY'S P.J.'S

Place on Fold

Center
Seam

FRONT
HERBY'S PAJAMAS

CUT 2

BACK
HERBY'S PAJAMAS

CUT 2

Center
Seam

D G

¼'' Seam Allowance

SLEEVE
HERBY'S PAJAMAS

CUT 2

½'' Seam Allowance

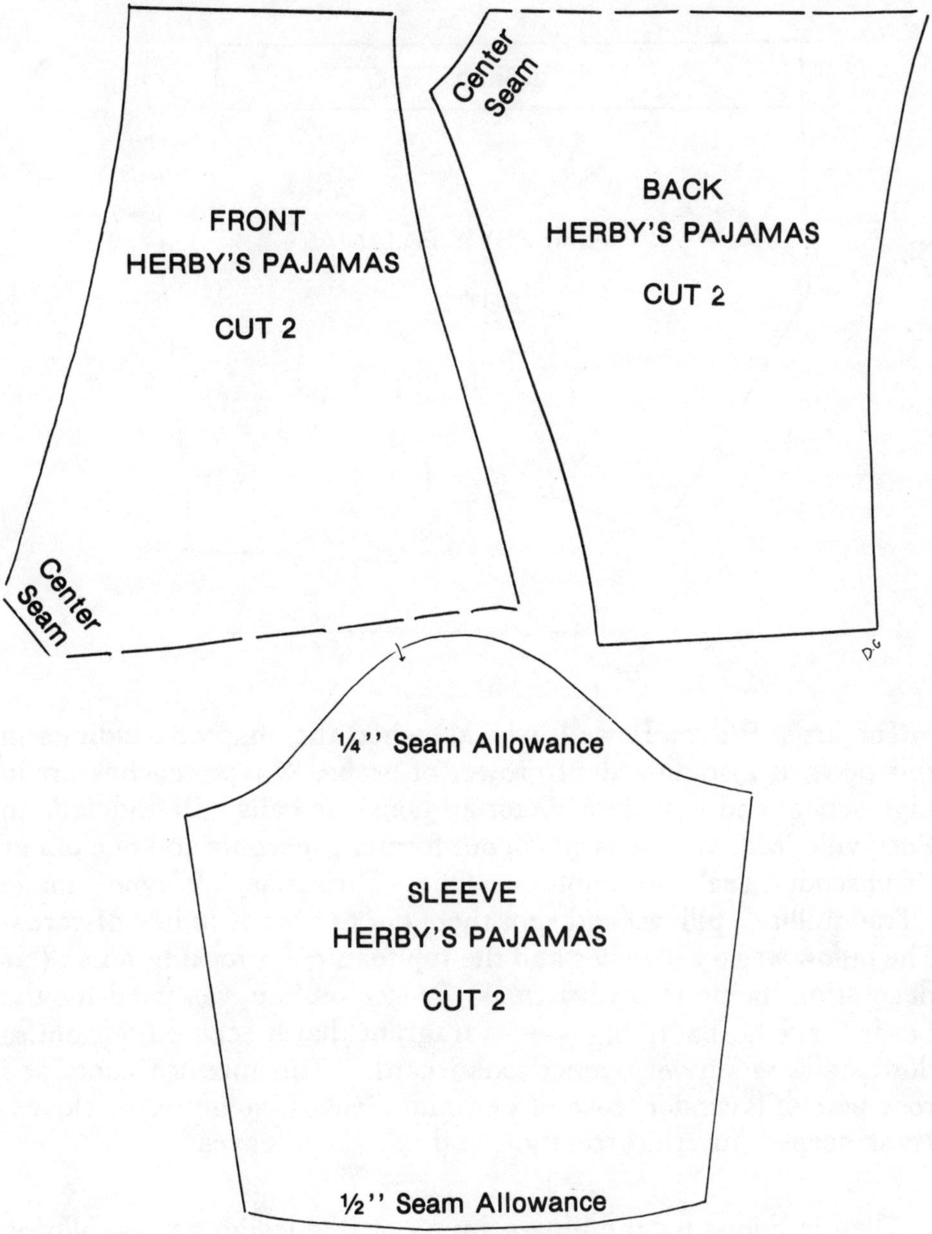

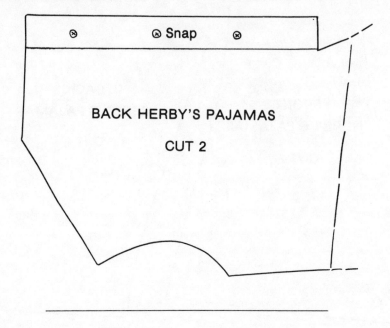

The artist Wayne Powell, who sketched the chapter headings in this book, is also an ardent grower of herbs. Wayne teaches art in high school and lives in a Victorian home he calls "Blythdale," in Perryville, Md. Wayne is one of our former cubscouts and one of our "Cubscout Tea" promoters. One Christmas, Wayne made "Tranquillity" pillows and sent them out to friends in lieu of cards. The pillow was 6 x 9 inches and the top featured a rocking horse (his decorating theme that Christmas). A lace outline was used for the border. The herbal filling was so fragrant that it scented our entire downstairs when we opened our "card." The mixture contained rose petals, lavender, rose of geranium leaves, some mint, cloves, frankincense, myrrh, orris root, and patchouli leaves.

The directions for the blue printing of the design are as follows:

BLUE PRINTING, A PHOTOGRAPHIC/CHEMICAL PROCESS ON CLOTH

> 1 ounce ferric ammonium citrate
> ½ ounce potassium ferricyanide
> 1 cup water
> wide-mouth glass jar
> old spoon
> strainer
> clean paint brush
> rubber gloves
> cotton cloth (thoroughly washed)

Steps: Wear rubber gloves. If chemicals get on your skin, it will turn bright blue (which, fortunately, eventually will fade).

1. Prepare solution:

A. Pour 1 cup of water in glass jar, add ½ ounce potassium ferricyanide, stir until dissolved.

B. Add 1 ounce ferric ammonium citrate, stir until dissolved.

C. Pour through strainer to remove lumps, and return to glass jar.

2. In a dimly lit room with the cloth on a moveable board, paint the cotton with the chemical solution. Fabric will turn chartreuse. A border may be made by laying a cardboard frame on the cloth.

3. Arrange dried or fresh flowers, ferns, or cut-out stencils on fabric. Plan interesting blank areas; delicate forms work better.

4. Carry the entire print out into direct bright sunlight, allow chemical to dry in the sun. The chemical first turns blue and then develops a slight brown haze. Be careful not to move the items on the cloth during this time.

5. Remove frame and plants; immediately wash cloth in cool water until the water runs clear. The under-developed chemical will wash out, the developed chemical is blue.

Herbal Hints

A List of Herbs,
their Culture
and some Common Uses

ANGELICA (*Angelica archangelica*) Common names—Masterwort and Holy Ghost plant. A biennial, it will grow to a height of 6 feet in moderate climate. It likes moist clay soil and partial shade. Flowers bloom in May, but do not let the seeds mature or the plant will die. According to legend, during the terrible plague in England, Michael the Archangel appeared in a vision to a monk and said that the plant would cure plague. At that time it grew in abundance in London. John Gerard says in his 1633 edition of *The Herbal*: "The roots of garden angelica is a singular remedy against poison and against the plague, and all infections taken by evill and corrupt aire," and he advised chewing the root to drive away "pestilentiall aire." All parts of the plant are used. Stems candied and for flavoring, leaves as tea, and roots as bread and as an ingredient in hop bitters. During the Middle Ages, candied angelica was a substitute for Alcohol Anonymous. Wives fed it to their husbands to

Angelica

cure the craving for intoxicating liqueurs and to instill a disliking for alcohol. The candied stems are used to decorate fruit cakes and are added to jellies. The fresh stems and leaves add flavoring to rhubarb dishes.

Anise

ANISE (*Pimpinella anisum*) Star Anise, Anise Star. Annual, Plant in light soil (does not transplant easily). Reaches a height of around 18 inches. Gerard says: "The seed is good against belchings and unbraidings of the stomacke—being chewed it makes the breath sweet and is good for them that are short winded, and quencheth thirst." Anise seeds are used as a spice, in sachets and in liqueurs. The leaves are used in salads; the oil for medicinal and antiseptic purposes. In early times, fishermen baited their fish hooks with anise and housewives would even use the seeds as bait in mousetraps.

Basil

BASIL (*Ocimun basilicum*) Sweet Basil, Kiss Me Nicholas, St. Joseph's Wort. Annual. Grows to 18 inches in height in ordinary garden soil. It is an herb that really gets around. The generic name is derived from *Oza*, a Greek word meaning odor. In France it is known as Herbe Royale. The Hindu plants basil by his doorway to ward off evil spirits. Gerard must have thought also along these lines, for he advises: "The juice mixed with fine meale of parched barley, oil of roses and vinegar is good against inflammations and the stinging of venomous beasts." To keep the plant from going to seed, clip off the flowering shoots. Uses: fresh or dried leaves are excellent with tomato dishes, cheese, omelets, soups and vinegar.

Bay

BAY (*Laurus nobilis*) Sweet Bay, True Laurel. Perennial. Plant in a wooden tub for convenience in bringing indoors during the winter. Needs moist soil. Bay leaves are associated with the making of laurels to crown victors and heroes in Ancient Greece and Rome. Bay is valued as a culinary herb. Added to boiling water in cooking shrimp, bay imparts a spicy taste. Use in soup stock, with liver, lamb, beef stews and goulash, with squash, spaghetti sauce, seafood and tomato aspic. A bay leaf kept in cannisters storing flour, corn meal and cereals will prevent invasion of those pesky little moths.

Balm

BALM (*Melissa officinalis*) Lemon Balm. Perennial which grows 2 feet in height. Gerard says it is useful planted in gardens where bees are kept because "they are delighted with this herbe above all others," and added, "when they are strayed away, they do finde their way home againe to it." Harvest the plant when the volatile oils are strongest. Dry in shade. Use fresh or dried in teas. A few leaves tucked under the upper crust of an apple pie gives a lemony flavor. Also used in sachets, perfumes and medicines.

Bergamot

BERGAMOT (*Monarda didyma*) Oswego Tea, Bee-Balm. A perennial which grows up to 4 feet in height in fertile soil. Has brilliant red flowers. Other varieties have pink, lavender and white flowers. In the Middle Ages, Knights of Old used bergamot as a rub-down after a bout of jousting. It is still an ingredient in some linaments and astringents. Early settlers used bergamot as a substitute for tea. The oil is used in perfume, soaps and sachets.

Borage

BORAGE (*Borago officinalis*) Bee Bread. A hardy annual which grows about 18 inches high in ordinary garden soil. Pliny called it "Euphrofinu—because "it maketh a man merry and joyful." And there is an old saying: "Borage brings alwaies courage." I wonder if both of these virtues are the results of its usage in making wine! The leaves have a slight cucumber taste and while small and tender are used in salads. The blossoms are bright blue with black stamens. Borage flowers were so admired in the Middle Ages that they were embroidered on royal robes. Today we use the blossoms in lemonade, in wines and candy them. Galen says the leaves and flowers are good for hoarseness and sore throat.

Burnet

BURNET (*Poterium sanguisorba*) Chaba's Salve. A perennial growing in clumps about 12 inches high. Has dark green serrated leaves. Gets the name Chaba's Salve from its healing properties discovered when a Hungarian King Chabairje used the juice to cure the wounds of 15,000 soldiers after a battle with his brother's army. The Chinese make use of its styptic qualities and the olden-day knights used the salve on their wounds. A far cry from the battle fields are its present-day usage; comfits and a gourmet wine vinegar.

Calendula

CALENDULA [*Calendula officinalis*] Marybud, Mary Gold, Pot of Marigold. Annual, but self sows. Grows 1 to 2 feet tall in ordinary garden soil, but likes sun. Gerard explains that the reason it is called Calendula is because it is to be seen in flower in the Calends almost of every month. He recommends: "conserve made of the floures and sugar taken in the morning fasting, cureth the trembling of the heart." He even suggests a meal using the petals in every dish on the menu. Grocers in the Netherlands keep a barrel of the petals to sell. They are used to color butter, flavor broths and other culinary purposes, as well as a medicine in healing salves, to cure toothache and in potpourri.

Camomile, Roman

CAMOMILE, ROMAN [*Anthemis nobilis*] Perennial. A creeping plant with fern-like foliage. When in bloom, camomile has small daisy-like flowers on 12-inch stems. The fragrance is likened to that of apple blossoms. It is often called the plant physician because it keeps plants growing near it healthy. Gerard attests to its healing virtues, and says that it is good against "collick and stone." Because of its mat-like growth, it makes a good groundcover and is often used on paths and kept mowed. Uses include teas, hair rinses, repellents and poultices.

Caraway

CARAWAY [*Carium carvi*] Homing Herb, Holding Herb. Biennial. Grows about 30 inches tall. If sown in the fall, the seeds may be harvested the following year. Gets the name "homing herb" because it brings homing pigeons back to the loft. Its name "holding herb" is because it is reputed to keep folks at home, This is a widely used herb in European countries and the Far East. Germans make a liqueur, Kummel, from it. They also use the seeds in sauerkraut, breads, cakes and cheese. It is customary in England to serve a dish of caraway seeds with apples. Used as a carminative, confectionery and in perfumes.

Catnip

CATNIP [*Nepeta Cataria*] Catmint. Perennial which likes dry sandy soil. Grows to 3 feet high and should be harvested as soon as it is mature. At one time, this herb was used as flavoring and some still recommend brewing a tea with a tablespoon of the herb to a cup of boiling water as a remedy for headaches or nervousness. It is also used as a bee forage. The principle use, however, is as Gerard says: "The later herbalists do call it Herba Cattani because the cats are very much delighted herewith, for the smell of it is so pleasant to them that they rub themselves upon it, and wallow or tumble in it, and also feed on the branches and leaves very greedily."

Chervil

CHERVIL [*Anthriscus cerefolium*] Annual. Grows about 19 inches in height and prefers partial shade. One of the herbs introduced in England by the Romans. A favorite salad herb, it is also one of the ingredients in fines herbes. Gerard says about chervil roots: "I do use to eate them with oil and vinegar, being first boyled, which is very good for old people that are dull and without lust and strenght." Besides all this, the oil extracted from its seeds is used in perfumes and as a polish for oak floors.

Chives

CHIVES [*Allium schoenophrasum*] Perennial. Chives can be started from seeds but this herb is usually propagated by dividing the clumps and planting the little bulbs. Six bulbs will produce a nice clump in one season. The more you use the plants, the more they produce. Clip leaves from one side at a time and not all over the plant, unless it is the final harvesting for the season. Grows in ordinary soil to about 10 inches high. Chives have a delicate onion flavor and are often used as a good substitue for those who cannnot tolerate onions. They dry and freeze well. I dry a few of the mauve clover-like blossoms to use in floral arrangements and press some for use in pictures. Chives are a pleasant addition to soups, omelets, potatoes, cream cheese and sour cream dips.

Comfrey

COMFREY [*Symphytum officinale*] Knitback, Knitbone, Healing Herb. A hardy perennial, comfrey likes rich soil and will grow as high as 5 feet. The leaves are quite large and resemble a donkey's ears. The blossom is mauve and hangs in little bells similar to Virginia Bluebell. Known for its healing properties (possibly the only plant to extract Vitamin B-12 from the soil), it contains potash, phosphate and calcium. It is also high in protein and fiber. The Japanese use the leaves in saunas by wrapping the body from chin to toes in the leaves, believing the skin will absorb the vitamins and minerals. Gerard says that if the roots of comfrey are stamped and the juice drank it will heal those "that spit blood and all inward wounds and burstings." He also recommends: "the same bruised and laid to in a manner of a plaister. doth heale all fresh and greene wounds and are so glutenatiuse, that it will sodder or glew together meate that is chopt in peeces seeting in a pot, and make it into one lumpe." This is quite a testimonial! We do know that it makes a good potherb if the smaller leaves are used and cooked as spinach. All parts of the plant are used: the roots in medicine, the leaves in cooking and as a poultice and blossoms french fried. It is a popular herbal tea for health enthusiasts.

Coriander

CORIANDER [*Coruandrum sativum*] An annual, it grows in sandy soil to about 3 feet in height. Although the Bible describes Manna as resembling coriander seed, Gerard calls it a "stinking herb." However, he adds that the dried seeds steeped in vinegar for 24 hours and then dried "causeth good digestion." It is used today in perfumery, coated with sugar as comfits, in flavoring custards, cakes, breads, vegetables and meats.

Costmary

COSTMARY [*Chrusanthemum balsamita*] Bible Leaf, Goosefoot. A perennial, costmary will grow up to 5 feet in height in sandy soil. A good background plant because of its size, it was a familiar herb in early American gardens. It is called Bible Leaf because the fragrant minty leaves were carried in the Bible as a bookmark. When the sermon got too long and the church-goer became drowsy, he could sniff on the leaf to stay awake. It is used in teas and sachets. Little bundles of costmary are used to sweeten the linen closet.

Dill

DILL [*Anthum graveolens*] An annual, it will re-seed itself if the bed is not disturbed. Dill thrives in a rich soil and will grow to a height of 3 feet. Because the plant matures quickly, it is wise to do successive planting. For some reason the dill and the cucumbers are never ready at the same time. I try to keep some of the seed heads and weed frozen to make sure I have them when needed. The umbels dried while still green are nice in floral arrangements. Dill is a versatile culinary herb. It is used in bread, pickles, with potatoes (mashed, fried and salad), in cole slaw, in apple pie and sprinkled on biscuits.

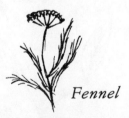

Fennel

FENNEL [*Foeniculum vulgare*] Sweet Fennel. A biennial, fennel should be sown in fertile soil and away from such plants as wormwood, caraway, bush beans and tomatoes. A tall plant, 4 or 5 feet, it will have some umbels the first year. The crop of seeds, however, will not be ready until the second year. The feathery foliage can be used anytime. It is especially good in a sauce with fish. Fennel has one particular "virtue" that appeals to most everyone nowadays—if you cook it in soups or chew the seeds, it will appease the appetite.

Feverfew

FEVERFEW (*Chrusanthemum parthenium*) Featherfew, Bride's Button. A perennial, it grows about 2 feet in height. Has a dainty white, daisy-like blossom, and bees are said to dislike this plant very much. A handful of the flowerheads carried where bees are will cause them to keep at a distance. It is attractive in borders and dries nicely for winter bouquets. It is used as a repellent and was once used prolifically as a medicine—a vermifuge, stimulant, tonic and carminative.

Garlic

GARLIC (*Allium sativum*) An ancient herb, garlic is a perennial and is propogated by sets. It grows over 2 feet in height and is a sprawly and unattractive plant. It can be partially hidden away where it will do the most good—around the grape harbor, along a fence or behind some rose bushes. Set out in early spring for fall harvest. Likes rich soil. We think of garlic in culinary terms, but it is also a powerful antiseptic.

Germander

GERMANDER (*Teucrium chamaedrys*) Wood Sage. Perennial, grows to 2 feet high and makes an attractive hedge around the herb garden. It has some medicinal uses. I press the curved stems when they are in flower to use in pressed flower pictures.

Horehound

HOREHOUND [*Marrubium vulgare*] Hoarhound. Perennial which can be found growing wild along roadsides. Thrives in poor soil and grows 2 feet in height. It is one of the bitter herbs mentioned in the Bible. The Romans carried horehound into the provinces when they were making their conquests. They depended on the herb to cure chest ailments and colds. It is still used in cough syrups and cough drops.

HORSERADISH [*Armoracia lapathifolia*] A perennial propogated by root division in early spring. Likes a clay-type soil and will grow to about 2 feet in height. The root is harvested in the fall, but I use it whenever my supply runs out. It is more potent in the fall.

Horseradish

Horseradish was used medicinally in early times as an irritant, to promote perspiration, and as a remedy for worms in children. Today it adds zest to cooking.

Hyssop

HYSSOP [*Hyssopus officinalis*] Perennial. Will thrive in ordinary soil. Grows 2 feet in height and makes a nice hedge. Some like the taste of hyssop leaves in salads. Medicinal uses include treatment of bruises and rheumatism. It can be mixed with sage as a gargle for a sore throat. The oil is used in making perfume.

Lavender

LAVENDER [*Lavandula vera: Lavandula spica*] Perennials. Several varieties are winter hardy in Appalachia—English lavender [*Augustifolis*]; Hidcote [*Angustifolis angustifolia vera*]   and Munstead (early blooming). Vera is a small shrub from 1 to 2 feet high and very aromatic. Spica is more dwarfish and furnishes the oil of Spike which is used in the preparation of artistical varnishes and employed by porcelain painters. This herb is sometimes difficult to establish. It needs lots of sun and does well if a little lime is worked into the soil. I place several flat rocks around my plants to give them protection and help them thrive. Lavender flowers should be picked before they open. They dry quickly and retain their fragrance. Uses include perfumes, aromatic stimulants, tonics and repellents.

Lemon Verbena

LEMON VERBENA [*Lippia citriodora*] Perennial. Should be planted in a tub so that it can be moved indoors during the winter. Needs a rich soil, full sun and must be kept watered. It is worth this special attention for it is delightful in sachets and potpourri. A leaf or two added to a cup of tea is delicious.

Lovage

LOVAGE [*Levisticum officinale*] Sea Parsley. A perennial which may grow as high as 6 feet in fertile soil. One plant will supply a family of four. Very pungent celery flavor. Used in soups, omelets, stuffings and salads. My grandchildren like to use the hollow stems as drinking straws. While a home economics teacher from Brussels, Belgium, was walking through my herb garden and trying to recognize some of the plants, she exclaimed when she saw the lovage: "This, I know, we candy the root."

Marjoram

MARJORAM [*Origanum majorana*] Annual. Needs a sweet soil and full sun and grows to 8 or 9 inches in height. Seeds should be started indoors in early spring. This is one of my favorite herbs—so fragrant and flavorful. Its uses are many: excellent seasoning for poultry, pork, lamb, sausage, hash, eggs, cottage cheese, to flavor herb butters, in teas and to add fragrance to potpourri and sweet bags.

Mint

MINT [*Mentha—numerous varieties*] Most mints are perennial and will germinate from seed in about 2 weeks. A plant purchased from a nursery will soon spread. In fact, mints should be contained by planting in 3-pound shortening or coffee cans with tops and bottoms removed or similar container, because the roots will take over one's garden. I raise apple, orange, lavender, pineapple, stone, mountain, white, Japanese, Jerusalem and Roman mint on the shady side of the house. The mints vary in flavor and strength, but for neat growth I prefer the orange, lavender and stone mints. Corsican, the smallest-leaved mint, is a creeping plant and one I have trouble establishing. Mints like moisture and grow quickly when planted near an outside water faucet. All mints are great as room fresheners (put some down the garbage disposal to dispel odors or in the fireplace). Mints have dozens of uses—it is a repellent to mice and other rodents (reason enough to plant it around the house); it is used in refreshing teas, in jelly, aromatic vinegars, with peas and carrots, lamb, fruits, in sweet waters, potpourri, as a moth repellent, in baths, as a "simple" to settle the stomach, and industrially in candy, chewing gum, cosmetics, cigarettes, mouthwash and deodorizers. Do plant some mint!

Nasturtium

NASTURTIUM [*Tropaeolum majus*] Annual which should be started early from seed in a well-drained and sunny spot. Soak the seeds in water for a couple of hours to hasten germination. Does well in hanging baskets and planters where it can vine. The flowers, leaves and seeds all have a peppery taste and are good on sandwiches and in salads. Makes a fine vinegar and, when the blossoms are finished, the seeds may be pickled and used as a substitute for capers.

Oregano

OREGANO [*Origanum—various species*] A perennial which grows about 2 feet in height and thrives in sun or partial shade. Sow seed early by merely pressing the seeds into the soil. It should germinate in 3 weeks. Thin plants to 12 inches apart. Once established, it will self-sow. This is the herb associated with pizza, spaghetti and other Italian specialities. Greek oregano [*prismaticum*] which can be purchased from a nursery, grows wild in Greece and Italy. It is more flavorful than the *vulgare* species. The name *origanium* means "ornament of the hills." Culpepper claimed that oregano juice dropped into the ears alleviates pain and noise in them and even helps deafness. The herb is mostly used in cooking and both varieties are good in soups, salads, tomato dishes, with fish and it has some use in potpourri.

Parsley

PARSLEY [*Petroselinum hortense and Petroselinum crispim*] A biennial, though I always treat it as an annual, wintering the plant and using it until the new crop matures. Will grow to a height of 10 inches in rich soil and partial shade. Soak seeds overnight and don't dispair when they don't pop right up through the ground. Some say the seeds must go to Hades and back seven times. There is an old saying: "If parsley seeds are sown in the haire three times a yeare, the haire will not fall out." This garnish, so often discarded, has much value nutritionally. It is very rich in vitamins A and C and iron. The Greeks did not use it in cooking as they considered parsley a medicine, but Greek charioteers fed parsley to their horses believing it gave them speed. Parsley can be harvested up until frost and is one of the herbs which dries easily. Use the oven method. Spread a layer of leaves on a cookie sheet and leave overnight in the oven with the pilot light on. They will be dry by the next morning. Check to be sure there is no moisture before sealing in an opaque jar. Parsley is a breath sweetener and parsley tea is often used by those who suffer with arthritis. Fresh parsley included in the daily diet is supposed to prevent the formation of kidney stones. Actually, we could devote an entire chapter to parsley, its superstitions and its benefits. It is an indispensable herb to the cook as one of the ingredients in fines herbes and bouquet garni, in salads, cooked in a butter sauce with new potatoes, in soups, stews and as a garnish.

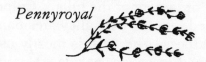

Pennyroyal

PENNYROYAL [*American—Hedeona puleogiorides; English—Mentha pulegium*] Perennials. The American pennyroyal grows 8 inches high and can be found growing wild in fields. It has an intense minty aroma and was a favorite medicinal herb of the Indians who used it for everything from stomach cramps to influenza. English pennyroyal is a low creeping mint with clover-like blossoms along the stems. It is the pennyroyal that is referred to as a flea repellent. Common names for American pennyroyal are squawmint and tickweed.

Rosemary

ROSEMARY [*Rosmarinus officinalis*] Perennial evergreen shrub which grows from 2 to 6 feet in height. Used down through the centuries in church ceremonies, both bridal and funeral. There is a legend that the bush grows to 6 feet in 33 years, the height of Christ in his life span. It may grow in width after this time but not in height. There is a saying: "Rosemary flourishes where the woman rules," however, it is definately a man's herb. The invigorating pine fragrance is appealing to men. Rosemary needs well-drained soil and likes the sun. It is supposed to strengthen the memory. It was used as an ingredient in the famous Hungary Water concocted by a hermit for Queen Elizabeth of Hungary who suffered from paralysis of the joints. Daily bathing in this water cured the queen. The receipt has been passed down through the years. The recipe recorded in *The Country Housewife and Lady's Director* (1732) calls for one handful of rosemary to every gallon of Brandy or clean Spirits, and one handful of lavender and about one handful of myrtle. "Put these to infuse in the Spirits and distill it, and you will have the finest Hungary Water that can be." In cooking, rosemary adds flavor to seafood, wines, egg dishes, all meats and poultry, for seasoning mashed potatoes and sprinkled over biscuits. The oil is used in medicines and the dried herb is an ingredient in potpourri and sachets.

Rue

RUE [*Ruta graveolens*] Herb of Grace. A perennial, rue grows in a mound shape from 2 to 3 feet in height. Thrives in ordinary soil but requires sunlight. Gerard had a high regard for rue saying the juice would protect one from the biting of serpents and stinging of scorpions. Rue was placed on the judges bench in courtrooms in early England to protect the judges from being infected with gaol fever, a prevalent ailment of the prisoners from Newgate. Rue is seldom used in cooking because of its strong taste. Its uses are medicinal and it is one of the recommended repellents.

Saffron

SAFFRON [*Crocus sativus*] Plant the bulbs in the spring for fall blooming. Each lavender blossom has three stigmas. These are picked and dried and used to season and color breads, rolls and rice. It takes some 60,000 stigmas to produce a pound, so this product is sometimes extended with pot marigold petals.

Sage

SAGE [*Salvia officinalis*] A perennial which grows 2 feet high, likes rich soil and full sun. Plants started from seed may be harvested the first year. Does well planted near rosemary. An old saying: "He who eats sage in May, will live for aye," is borne out by records of people who lived to be quite old and attributed their longevity to eating sage. Chinese prefer sage to their own tea. The aspirin of the early settlers were pills made of sage, tallow and honey. Sage tea makes a good hair rinse. Several varieties of sage add interest to the herb garden: Clary [*Salvia sclarea*] is a tall, showy herb; *Salvia elegens* and *clevelandii* are both very fragrant and the leaves are used in sachets.

Santolina

SANTOLINA [*Santolina chamaecyparissus* Such a long name for a dainty little plant whose foliage resembles sea coral. There is another variety, *Santolina viridis,* which is green with a grasslike growth. The former santolina, referred to as lavender cotton, makes a nice edging for use in knot and formal herb gardens. I use them in my rose garden to repel insects and dry the foliage to use in pressed pictures and flower arrangements. They have no culinary value.

Scented Geraniums

SCENTED GERANIUMS [*Pelargonium graveolens*] A tender perennial which must be brought indoors during the winter months. This is the geranium which I prefer to use in cooking and in potpourri featuring a strong rose scent. Prince Rupert *crispum* has a strong lemon scent; Pungent Peppermint *tomentosum* has velvety leaves shaped like grape leaves; all are excellent in flavoring jelly, cakes, sugar, in potpourri, sachets and slumber pillows. There are so many varieties of scented geraniums I will not try to list them, however, the nurseries listed in the back of the book can supply a wide choice of this delightful herb.

Southernwood

SOUTHERNWOOD [*Artemisia abrotanum*] Lad's Love. Perennial which grows from 2 to 5 feet in height. Has a pungent aroma. Boys would rub the foliage on their faces believing it would grow a beard. An excellent moth repellent, the bush-like plant is also attractive in landscaping. There are several varieties; some have a lemon odor, a camphor odor or tangerine. A southernwood tea is considered sophoric and a tiny bit can be added to beet soup.

Summer Savory

SUMMER SAVORY [*Satureja hortensis*] The Bean Herb. Annual which grows to 18 inches in height. Sow outdoors when ground is warm. Likes full sun and a little lime in the soil. The herb is most aromatic and is used with meats, fish, poultry, meatloaf, eggs, stuffings and gives a zesty flavor to all bean dishes. *WINTER SAVORY [montana]* is a hardy perennial with dark and shiny leaves. It is used as a condiment and in some liqueurs. Propogate by cuttings. Summer savory should be staked since it begins to collapse when it reaches full growth.

Sweet Woodruff

SWEET WOODRUFF [*Asperula odorata*] Master of the Wood. A perennial which likes shade. This is one herb which will thrive when planted beneath trees. Grows about 8 inches high and resembles My Lady's Bedstraw. It has small white flowers set on a slender stalk with narrow leaves growing round it in successive whorls. A popular herb in Germany where it is known as Waldmeister and Magerkraut. Sprigs of the herb were once carried into battle by the old Teuton warriors as a charm. It is widely used to scent stored clothing. The fragrance (that of vanilla) is quite lasting. Woodruff is best known for its use in flavoring and aromatizing a variety of beverages. For example, the Maibowle which is traditionally drunk on May 1 in Germany. Other uses are tisanes and syrups. It is easily dried.

Tansy

TANSY [*Tanacetum vulgare*] Bitter Buttons, Stinking Willie. A perennial which reaches the height of 4 feet. Tansy is one of the bitter herbs. Tansy cakes and tansy puddings were eaten at Easter in earlier times and is still a custom in some parts of England. Tansy tea was a ''simple'' for allaying pains of childbirth. It was also used as an embalming agent in ancient days. Thrives in ordinary soil and like mint, should have its roots contained. Best known as a repellent. The fern tansy is smaller in height and a more attractive plant.

Tarragon

TARRAGON [*Artemisia dracunculus*] Perennial which grows 20

inches high, likes full sun but not too much water. A favorite herb in French cooking. According to the doctrines of signatures, because the roots resemble coiling serpents, it was believed the plant would draw the venom from snake bites. It was used by the pilgrims in the Middle Ages. They believed a sprig of tarragon in their shoes would give them stamina on their trip to the Holy Land. Today's uses are culinary: tarragon vinegar, use with beets, vegetables, fish, poultry, eggs, white sauces.

Thyme

THYME [*Thymus vulgaris*] Perennial which grows to the height of 8 inches in soil sweetened with a little lime. I place flat rocks for the plants to clamber over. There are numerous varieties—wooly, French, English, nutmeg, caraway, to name just a few. It was a favorite herb of the Greeks who used it as a rubdown after bathing. It is said to be one of the herbs that was in the manger when Christ was born and for this reason is used in creches on Christmas. Bees are greatly attracted to thyme. A design featuring a bee hovering over a sprig of thyme was embroidered on pennants by many a lady for her knight—it symbolized courage. Though thyme is used in treating colds and has other medicinal uses, we like it in cooking. The old saying: "No good cook is ever without thyme" is certainly true. Thyme is good in just about everything. Two sprigs of thyme steeped in warm milk, the milk strained and added to mashed potatoes, is subtle and delicious.

WORMWOOD [*Artemisia absinthium*] Absinth. A perennial which grows about 2 feet high in poor soil. It is one of the bitter herbs and is used in linaments, as a vermifuge and as an insect

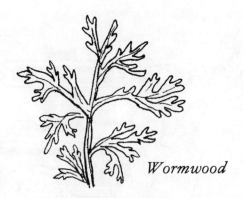

Wormwood

repellent. A tiny bit used with roast goose will counteract the fat.

Yarrow

YARROW [*Achillea millefolium*] A perennial which prefers sun and does well in ordinary soil. Repels Japanese beetles, flies and ants. The flowers, which are bright golden yellow, are much used in dried arrangements. White yarrow also drys easily, however the rose blossoming yarrow does better when dried using a medium such as silica gel or borax.

Granny's In The Kitchen!

When our children were small, we lived near the school and they would walk home for lunch. Their frequent request on leaving home in the morning was: "Mom, bake some cookies today so we can smell them when we're walking down the street." Those were the Cookie Days, and I miss them!

Most of us have memories of fresh bread baking in the oven, tomato catsup simmering on the stove, sassafras tea brewing in a pot, and apple butter bubbling in a big brass kettle as the women of the neighborhood took turns stirring and replenishing the wood fire built in the backyard. Using herbs in meal preparation will bring back some of those nostalgic aromas.

If you grow your own herbs—great! However, dried herbs may be used instead (after all, we hope you raise so many herbs that you will have plenty to dry for winter use). In our recipes we give the amount for fresh herbs, sometimes using sprigs (2-inch tips of the herb plant), sometimes a handful, but usually standard measurements. In this case, use ½ as much of the dried herb. When available, buy the the herb in leaf form and then powder it between the palms of the hands when adding it to the dish. To get the full benefit from the a tea strainer and plunge into hot boiling water; leave for 10 seconds and then plunge the herb into cold water for 10 seconds. amount of time.

The recipes that follow are family favorites. Some have been passed down by word-of-mouth, others have been given to us by friends. We like them and hope that you will too.

Appetizers

HOMOS BI TAHINI

1 can (20 ounces) chick peas, blended
2 tablespoons Tahini paste (roasted hulled sesame seeds available in a can in most supermarkets).
1 teaspoon lemon juice
1 tablespoon olive oil
Dash salt

Drain chick peas. Place in blender with lemon juice, Tahini paste, olive oil and dash of salt. Blend. Serve with Syrian bread cut in 2-inch pieces (Pita Bread).

ZIPPY DIP

Mix in blender two 3-ounce packages cream cheese, 1 teaspoon horseradish, ½ teaspoon prepared mustard, 1 teaspoon Worcestershire sauce, 2 drops hot sauce, 2 tablespoons pickle relish, 3 tablespoons chili sauce. Yields 1 cup.

FRESH HERB DIP

Combine ½ cup cottage cheese, ½ cup sour cream and 1 teaspoon each of the following fresh herbs (finely chopped): sweet basil, chives, dill weed, lovage leaves, thyme, parsley, tarragon and chervil. Season lightly with salt and a grind of fresh pepper. Let stand in refrigerator for several hours before serving. This is a good dip for raw vegetables.

EGGPLANT APPETIZER

1 medium eggplant (about 1 pound), cut into
    bite-sized chunks
½ cup water
¼ cup olive or salad oil
1 tablespoon lemon juice
½ teaspoon salt
Four pitas (pocket breads)
1 tablespoon finely chopped Italian parsley
½ teaspoon chopped basil
2 grinds black pepper

Fry peeled eggplant in the olive oil for 3 minutes, stirring constantly. Add water and reduce heat to low. Cover and let simmer until eggplant is tender (about 10 minutes). Mash with fork, beat in lemon juice, parsley, basil and seasonings. Refrigerate.

Before serving, place pitas on cookie sheet and toast for 5 minutes, turning once. Cut each pita into 8 wedges. Guests spread the dip on the pitas. Makes 2 cups of dip and will spread 32 servings. (Note—a recipe for Pita Bread is included in this chapter).

Sandwiches

CHIVE-CHEESE SPREAD

This is a very simple recipe and is especially delicious when served on whole wheat bread. Soften 1 package of cream cheese with milk and mayonnaise until a spreadable consistency. Add chopped fresh chives and finely chopped pecans. If the bread slices are trimmed after being put together, it will make a neater sandwich.

CHIVE-PINEAPPLE SPREAD

One package of cream cheese softened with a little pineapple juice and mayonaise. Add drained crushed pineapple and chopped chives.

TANGY EGG SPREAD

Mix together 4 minced hard-cooked eggs, 3 strips crisp bacon, crumbled, 1 teaspoon horseradish, 1 teaspoon minced shallots (onion may be substituted), 1 teaspoon Worcestershire sauce, ¼ cup mayonnaise, ¼ teaspoon salt. Yields 1 cup.

FRIZZLED BEEF 'N CHEESE

1 large can chipped beef cut into small pieces

½ cup mild cheddar cut into cubes
6 shallots (medium), minced, or 1 medium onion, chopped
1 green pepper, chopped
¼ stick margarine
4 slices regular bread

Saute shallots and green pepper in margarine. Add the beef and let it get a little curley on the edges. Now add the cheese and when it begins to melt, lay the slices of bread over the mixture. Use a large skillet for this recipe and remove the sandwiches with a pancake turner. This is a "quickie" when you are too frazzled to get a meal. It is filling and all you will need is a beverage and some fruit to round out the menu.

WATERCRESS-WALNUT SANDWICHES

1 bunch watercress
¼ cup black walnuts, chopped
1 package (8 oz.) Neufchatel cheese which you soften
¼ teaspoon salt
4 slices of rye-caraway bread or thin pumpernickel

Chop the watercress (reserve a few sprigs for garnish). Add to the cheese along with the salt and walnuts. Spread mixture on bread. Cut diagonally in half and garnish with extra cress.

WELSCH-RAREBIT

1 pound sliced bacon
2 firm ripe tomatoes
1 egg
1 cup milk
2 tablespoons margarine
¾ teaspoon salt
¾ teaspoon dry mustard
¼ teaspoon paprika
3 cups sharp cheese, grated
¼ cup flour

Use a heavy saucepan or double boiler. Melt margarine, add flour and blend and gradually add 1 cup milk. Beat egg and mix with a little of the hot milk mixture and put into pan with the seasonings. Stirring constantly, add the cheese and cook gently until it is melted.

Toast four slices of bread. Place bacon on bread, then tomatoes and top with the cheese sauce. Garnish with minced fresh basil. For a heartier sandwich add sliced onions and sliced green pepper. Leftover cheese sauce may be used in scalloped potatoes.

OLD-FASHIONED PIMIENTO CHEESE

1 pound medium cheddar cheese (may use part longhorn)
½ pint canned pimientos
½ teaspoon vinegar
2 tablespoons brown sugar
¼ cup mayonnaise (may need to add more to make spreadable)

Grind together the cheese and pimientos. Add vinegar. Combine brown sugar with the mayonnaise and add to the mixture. Some of the juice from the pimientos may be added for more flavor.

HORSERADISH

No longer must we weep making horseradish—the blender has taken away the tears and made a quick job out of a frustrating chore. We raise our own horseradish and make it up fresh whenever it is needed. Some people say that it should be dug in the fall, and others hold to spring. We find there is no difference in quality at any season.

I prefer the smaller side shoots, though they are a bit tedious to peel. If you must buy the roots, it will take about a pound to make 3 cups.

Peel the roots with a potato peeler and chop into half-inch pieces. Put into electric blender with 1 cup white vinegar, 1 teaspoon salt, 2 teaspoons white sugar and a little water (about ¼ cup). Blend gradually, scraping the horseradish down from the sides with a spatula. I keep a pint jar in the refrigerator for present use and freeze the rest.

Horseradish adds zip to many dishes. Try a teaspoon in the dressing when mixing cole slaw or in salmon cakes. Some horseradish fans eat it three times a day. Yes, even for breakfast—on eggs.

CANAPE IDEAS

Fill a cookie press with pimiento, sharp or blue cheese and decorate bread strips for little open-faced sandwiches. Sprinkle with poppy seeds or nuts. Pat gently.

Trim crusts from French bread in oval pieces. Butter the crusts. Sprinkle with chive salt and minced parsley.

Spread bread with peanut butter. Dip edges in peanuts or herb jelly. Cheese spread bread dipped in minced parsley, chervil or chives can be topped with sliced olives.

Bread

RYE-CARAWAY BREAD

2 tablespoons caraway seed
2½ cups medium rye flour
2 packages active dry yeast
⅓ cup firmly packed brown sugar
1 tablespoon salt

Combine above ingredients and blend in mixer. Now heat over low heat to a very warm temperature (120-130 degrees) the following:

2 cups water
¼ cup sorghum or plain molasses
¼ cup margarine

Add to the flour mixture. Blend at low speed until moistened and continue blending for 2 more minutes at medium speed. Stir in 3½ to 4 cups all purpose flour (not self-rising) to form sticky dough. Put on kneading board and add ½ to ⅓ cup white flour until the dough is smooth and pliable and no longer sticky. Place dough in greased bowl. Cover and let rise in warm place until light (about 45 minutes). Grease two 8 x 4-inch loaf pans. Punch down dough and divide into 2 parts. Shape into rectangular loaves for loaf pan. Let rise in warm place until light but not quite doubled in size (30-40 minutes). Brush loaves with beaten egg before baking. Bake at 375 degrees for 25 to 30 minutes, or until loaf sounds hollow when lightly tapped. Immediately remove from pans and cool. This bread has a sweet flavor. You won't believe how many compliments you will get when you serve it.

HARMONY ACRES BREAD

1 package active dry yeast
2 cups milk, scalded
2 teaspoons salt
2 tablespoons savory leaves
4 teaspoons marjoram leaves
1 teaspoon oregano leaves
¼ cup warm water
2 tablespoons sugar
1 tablespoon margarine
3 teaspoons thyme leaves
5¾ to 6½ cups sifted all purpose flour

Soften yeast in warm water (110 degrees). Combine scalded milk, margarine, sugar and salt and let cool to lukewarm.

Add the crumbled herbs to 2 cups of flour and stir into the above liquid. Then add the softened yeast and mix. Add enough of the remaining flour to make a moderately stiff dough. Turn out on lightly floured bread board and knead till smooth and satiny (about 10 minutes). Shape into a ball; place in lightly greased bowl—turning over to grease surface. Cover and let rise in warm place till double in bulk (about an hour). Shape into 2 loaves and place in greased 9'' x5'' loaf pans. Oil top of loaf. Bake in hot oven (400 degrees) 35 minutes or till done. If tops brown too fast, cover loosely with foil the last 20 minutes.

For a variety, try other herb combinations: 2 teaspoons celery seed, 1 teaspoon powdered sage and ½ teaspoon ground nutmeg for each loaf.

SYRIAN BREAD [Pita]

9 cups all purpose flour
1 teaspoon salt
2 packages (14 ounces each)
    active dry yeast
3 cups potato water
¼ cup olive oil
¼ cup sugar
1 cup corn meal or flour

Pour ¼ cup of lukewarm potato water in a bowl and sprinkle with yeast and sugar. Let stand several minutes and stir to dissolve the yeast. Set bowl in a warm place free from drafts for 5 minutes (I use my oven which is slightly warm from the pilot light).

Combine flour and salt in a deep bowl. Make a well in the center and pour in yeast mixture, olive oil and the remaining potato water. Gently stir ingredients in center and incorporate them with the flour. Work with your fingers until the dough can be gathered into a compact bowl. Knead. Put into an oiled bowl and return to lukewarm oven for 2 hours or until dough has doubled in bulk. Punch dough down and divide into 8 pieces of equal size. Roll each piece into a ball about 2½ inches in diameter. Cover with a towel and let rest half an hour.

Lightly flour your bread board and roll the balls into 8-inch rounds 1/8 inch thick. Keep them flat. Arrange them 2 to 3 inches apart on baking sheets sprinkled with the corn meal or flour. Cover with a towel and let rest for 30 minutes. Bake in 500 degree oven on lowest shelf for 5 minutes, then on second shelf for 3 minutes until loaves are puffed and browned over. Remove bread from baking sheets and wrap each loaf in aluminum foil. Let rest 10 minutes and unwrap. You will find that the tops have fallen and there is a shallow air pocket in the center. The pockets are filled with spreads and used as sandwiches, or the pita is cut into small pieces and used with the eggplant and homos dips.

Because the loaves take up a lot of space—2 cookie sheets, we bake the loaves 4 at a time.

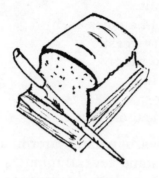

DILLY BREAD

1 package active dry yeast
¼ cup warm water
¼ teaspoon baking soda
2 ¼ to 2 ½ cups all purpose flour
1 cup cream-style cottage cheese
1 teaspoon onion flakes
¼ cup shortening
2 tablespoons white sugar
1 well-beaten egg
1 teaspoon salt
2 teaspoons dill seed and dill weed

Soften yeast in warm water. Heat cottage cheese to lukewarm and stir in shortening, sugar, onion flakes, the dill, salt, baking soda and softened yeast. Beat in egg and add flour a little at a time to make a soft dough. Knead on lightly floured surface till smooth and elastic. Place in greased bowl, turning to grease surface. Cover and let rise in warm place an hour. Punch down, cover, let rest 10 minutes and then shape into loaf pan. Cover and let rise again until almost doubled. Bake in 350 degree oven for 40 minutes. Remove from pan. Brush with melted butter and sprinkle with additional dill seed. Makes 1 loaf. This bread freezes well, so I usually double the recipe.

ROSEMARY ROLLS

2 packages active dry yeast
¼ cup lukewarm water
4 tablespoons sugar
2 teaspoons salt
2 cups buttermilk
¼ teaspoon soda
4 tablespoons melted shortening
5 cups all purpose flour (sifted)
2 tablespoons dried rosemary
3 tablespoons softened margarine

Heat the buttermilk slowly over low heat until it is lukewarm. Sprinkle yeast over the buttermilk. Add salt, sugar, soda and shortening. Mix well. Gradually add the flour, enough to make a soft dough. Turn out on lightly floured board and knead until satiny. Flatten dough and cut out rounds with biscuit cutter. Brush each round with the softened margarine and sprinkle with rosemary. Mark through the center with the back of a knife and fold over. Place rolls in a greased shallow pan 1 inch apart. Cover and let set in warm place to rise until double in bulk. Bake in hot oven 400 degrees from 15 to 20 minutes. Makes 6 dozen small rolls.

TOASTED SESAME or POPPY SEED

Omit the rosemary; instead, after shaping the rolls in pan, brush tops with milk. Sprinkle with 1½ tablespoons toasted sesame seed or poppy seed. Do not brush with butter. Let rise and bake 15 minutes.

OREGANO ROLLS

Oregano incorporated into the basic roll mixture above (with the flour; 3 teaspoons dried or 6 fresh, finely minced oregano) and shaped like buns is great for hamburgers.

MARJORAM BISCUITS

Marjoram is described as "sweet marjoram;" certainly fitting, as this is one of the most fragrant and flavorful herbs; a little bit of marjoram helps most any dish and its subtle flavor in hot biscuits—ummmm, is mouth watering!

The following recipe is basic and the biscuits are not only a good bread accompaniment to the meal, they are great for the "pouring over" of creamed chicken, tuna, etc. A commercial biscuit mix may also be used.

    2 cups flour
    4 teaspoons baking powder
    ½ teaspoon salt
    4 tablespoons shortening
    ¾ cup milk
    2 teaspoons dried marjoram

Sift flour, baking powder and salt together. Work in shortening with pastry blender or rub in with fingertips. Add milk slowly and then the marjoram. Mix to a soft dough. Roll out on a slightly floured board to ½-inch thickness. Cut with a biscuit cutter (or the floured edge of a glass) and bake in quick oven (450 degrees) 10 to 15 minutes. Yield: 12 biscuits.

BASIL CORN BREAD

Corn bread is another favorite at our house and, as most of us know, it has as affinity with soup beans. Why is it that hot bread served with any meal puts it into company fare? A simple salad, a plate of well-seasoned soup beans with a bit of ham, a fresh fruit and beverage and you have a meal that practically prepares itself. Actually, I like to put the beans on to simmer during days when I am working outside all day. Now to the recipe—

    1 cup yellow cornmeal
    1 cup sifted all purpose flour
    ½ teaspoon soda
    1 teaspoon baking powder

1 teaspoon dried basil
1 unbeaten egg
1 cup buttermilk
2 tablespoons shortening
1 tablespoon sugar

Stir buttermilk into cornmeal and let set. Sift other ingredients together. Add unbeaten egg, shortening and basil to buttermilk mixture and beat in the dry ingredients. Pour into greased skillet and bake about 25 minutes.

USE YOUR OWN RECIPES!

Most recipes are adaptable for herb breads, so if you have a favorite recipe, try adding some herbs for flavor. As we keep saying, "Use your imagination!" Being a creative cook is being adventurous. Such gourmet delights as waffles with a touch of thyme , dumplings with the savor of savory, spoonbread with rosemary—oh, my, the combinations are endless!

DEVILED EGGS "MIT" HERBS
6 large hard-cooked eggs

¼ teaspoon salt
½ teaspoon sugar
3 tablespoons mayonnaise
½ teaspoon minced shallots (may be omitted) and paprika
1 sprig fresh tarragon, minced
1 teaspoon prepared mustard
1 teaspoon tarragon vinegar
½ teaspoon margarine, softened

Halve peeled eggs and remove yolks. Mash yolks with margarine, add vinegar, spices and mayonnaise. Fill egg white cavities and sprinkle with paprika.

The herb flavor of the deviled eggs may be varied by substituting parsley, marjoram, thyme, or chervil for the tarragon. If this is the case, use plain cider vinegar.

CREAMED EGGS

½ stick margarine
¼ cup flour
6 large hard-cooked eggs
½ teaspoon curry powder
1 teaspoon salt (chive salt if available)
½ teaspoon dried marjoram or 2 teaspoons if fresh
Dash of Worcestershire sauce

Melt margarine, blend in flour and gradually add milk. Cook until creamy consistency. Add salt, marjoram, curry powder and sauce. Then gently add the sliced eggs.

The creamed eggs may be served on toast or chow mein noodles. For a complete luncheon or supper dish, place fresh or canned asparagus spears on toast slices, pour over the creamed eggs and top with crisp bacon.

QUICHE LORRAINE

Whether you serve it as a main course or cut into small pieces with drinks, quiche will fill the bill. Here again we give a basic recipe;

vary with different cheeses, vegetables and herbs.

  ½ pound bacon
  1 tablespoon margarine
  ½ cup finely cut shallots or onions
  3 eggs, slightly beaten
  1 tablespoon minced fresh parsely
  Pie crust for 1 shell
  2 cups top milk (some cream will make it richer)
  1 teaspoon salt
  ½ pound grated cheese of your choice
  Sprinkle of nutmeg or cayenne

Prepare pie crust or use a mix. Fry bacon crisp, crumble and set aside. Sauté the shallots or onions in margarine for 5 minutes. Mix other ingredients. Add bacon and shallots. Sprinkle with nutmeg or paprika. Pour into pie shell or flan pan lined with pastry and bake 10 minutes at 450 degrees, then reduce heat to 325 degrees and cook until firm. Cut into wedges. Canadian bacon or ham may be substituted for the bacon.

OMELET aux FINES HERBES

If you have a regular omelet pan, great, otherwise use a heavy cast aluminum skillet which will accomodate 4 eggs.

Beat 4 eggs slightly and add 4 tablespoons water, ½ teaspoon salt, choice of herbs. Melt 2 tablespoons margarine in hot omelet pan and when the butter begins to sizzle, add the eggs and reduce the heat. As the omelet cooks, lift it with a spatula to allow the uncooked part to run under until the omelet is creamy. Increase the heat to brown the under part. Fold double and turn onto hot serving platter. Herbs to add could be ½ teaspoon fresh minced parsley, chives, tarragon, and basil.

Salads

MACARONI SALAD

2 cups macaroni, cooked and cooled
1 tablespoon chopped onion
½ cup chopped celery
¼ cup chopped lovage with leaves
2 tablespoons chopped parsley
¼ cup thinly sliced raw carrots
½ cup chopped sweet pickles
½ cup cubed cheddar or longhorn cheese
2 tablespoons chopped pimientoes
1 cup mayonnaise

Combine above ingredients and chill well-covered in refrigerator. Garnish with hard-cooked egg slices, extra pimiento and parsley. The cubed cheese and lovage make it deliciously different.

POTATO SALAD

Eye appeal is something to go for when using white vegetables and pasta. This salad is hearty and colorful.

5 cups boiled potatoes
1 cup diced celery
1 green pepper, chopped

1 pimiento fresh or canned, chopped
1 teaspoon salt
1 teaspoon chopped onion (fresh green onions are good)
5 hard-cooked eggs
¼ cup chopped lovage
1 teaspoon minced dill weed
¼ cup vinegar
2 teaspoons sugar
1 cup mayonnaise (may need more to make moist)

Peel potatoes and dice into cubes. Pour vinegar over the warm potatoes and let marinate while you are getting the other ingredients ready, also add salt at this time. Blend the sugar into the mayonnaise. Add the other ingredients (except the sliced hard-cooked eggs) and the mayonnaise. The last step is to lightly toss the eggs with the other ingredients. Garnish the top with daisies—slices of hard-cooked egg whites centered with a yellow yolk. Parsley is used for leaves. Pimiento strips here and there in the daisy bouquet add more color.

BEAN SALAD

Marinating is the secret of really good bean salad. Mix the following:

½ cup white vinegar (try some of your herb vinegars for variety)
½ cup Safflower oil
1 cup sugar
1 teaspoon minced parsley
½ teaspoon minced lovage leaves
1 teaspoon salt
1 teaspoon fresh minced tarragon
1 teaspoon fresh minced basil
½ teaspoon dry mustard
½ teaspoon dill seed or weed
½ teaspoon minced marjoram

Heat and pour over the following:
      1 medium size can green beans
      1 medium can yellow (wax) beans
      1 medium can red kidney beans
      1 medium can large lima beans
      1 thinly sliced onion
      1 can black-eyed peas
      1 small can garbanzo beans
      1 small can of sliced water chestnuts
      1 green pepper, chopped
Refrigerate at least 4 hours or, better still, overnight. Just before serving, add the thinly sliced onion rings. The red Italian onions are sweet and colorful. Serve in bowl lined with lettuce leaves. I know this includes a lot of ingredients, but it is *one* hearty salad.

QUICK VEGETABLE SALAD
Chop into equal proportions fresh tomatoes, green peppers, onions and cucumbers. Make a dressing of vinegar diluted with water, sugar and salt and pour over the vegetables. Chill and serve with fresh chopped basil leaves.
      Tomato slices topped with chopped chives, chopped green onions, minced parsley or basil, and with a simple dressing of diluted vinegar, sugar and salt, or just a dollop of mayonnaise is a quick and nutritious salad.

FRUIT SALADS
Herbs which go nicely with fruit salads are any of the mints, a few thyme blossoms, clove pinks, lavender flowers, chopped rose petals, anise and borage blossoms.

Vegetables

Herb buters, vinegars and herb salts are standbys in seasoning vegetables, but for some more explicit recipes we will list some of the everyday types of vegetables served.

FRESH GREEN BEANS

Grandmother's string beans which simmered with a big chunk of salt pork on the back of the stove from morn till supper time had a delicious steaming aroma, but much of the nutrients evaporated with the steam and the salt pork did not help the waistline. Try the following recipe which leaves the beans crispy tender and a good shade of green.

    3 pounds fresh green beans
    7 quarts of water
    3½ tablespoons salt (added to water)
    3 tablespoons safflower oil
    3 sprigs of savory
    grind of pepper

Bring the water to boil in large kettle. Drop beans into kettle and bring the water back to boiling. Cook uncovered for 8 to 10 minutes (check for doneness, should be crunchy but tender). Drain in colander and run cold water over them to set the color. About 10 minutes before serving time, heat the oil in a skillet, add the beans, savory, pepper and toss. More salt may be needed. Heat gently and thoroughly. Remove savory sprigs and serve.

KOLOKITHAKIA YAHNI [*HERB STUFFED SQUASH*]

Every gardener seems to be overwhelmed with squash, especially the zucchini. This is a Greek recipe for preparing it.

2 lbs. small, firm zucchini
¼ cup butter
½ teaspoon crushed peppermint
1 medium sized onion
1 teaspoon sweet basil
salt to taste, grind of pepper

Wash squash, trim off ends, cut into ½-inch rounds. Slice onion into thin rings. Saute squash and onion in butter; sprinkle with salt, basil, peppermint and pepper. Cook only until just tender. Serve at once.

NEW POTATOES

Scrub and scrape the thin skins from new potatoes; put into saucepan with water to cover. Salt and then boil until done. The water should have boiled down quite a bit. Add margarine or butter and one of the following herbs, chopped—parsley, dill or chives (fresh, of course).

CARROTS WITH MINT

Slice scraped carrots into pan with a small amount of water. Cook quickly (do not overcook). Serve with a sauce made of 1 tablespoon margarine, 2 tablespoons chopped mint and a tablespoon of lemon juice.

OTHER COMBINATIONS

Green beans seasoned with lovage leaves; use rosemary butter on green beans; add basil wine vinegar to cooked red cabbage; season new peas with parsley and marjoram; cauliflower with basil; squash with dill; eggplant with marjoram and, of course, tomatoes with basil.

POTATOES AND HERBS

Herbs are a natural with potatoes. Try baking 4 large potatoes, scoop out the insides and add to this pulp: 3 tablespoons margarine, ¼ cup grated cheese, a little condensed milk, salt and 1 teaspoon of fresh thyme. Retun to shell, sprinkle more cheese on top and brown under broiler.

Thyme also goes well with mashed potatoes. Add 2 sprigs of fresh thyme or ½ teaspoon dried thyme to the hot milk; let steep 5 minutes and strain out thyme before adding milk to potatoes.

A pinch of marjoram or savory goes with just about any vegetable.

STUFFED FLANK STEAK

Salt, pepper and lightly flour flank steak. Make a stuffing of toasted bread crumbs, onions, celery and lovage sauteed in a little margarine. Mix with crumbs and add a sprig of fresh sage or 1 teaspoon of powdered sage. Season with salt and spread on the steak. Roll the steak and secure it with skewers and twine.

Brown on all sides in electric skillet. Add a small amount of water, cover and let steam until tender. Serve with mashed potatoes.

SPICED BEEF

I won't give any specified amount, but use a rump roast. Cover with cold water and when it comes to a boil, drain off water and scum and replace with a small amount of fresh water. Stick several cloves into the meat. Add a bay leaf, ¼ cup vinegar, ¼ cup brown sugar, 4 peppercorns and salt. Cover and cook slowly until tender.

HAMBURGERS

Herbs add zip to a plain old hamburger. Use ¼ pound of ground lean beef for each serving and bind with a beaten egg. To 1 pound of hamburger try the following combinations:

A small can of chopped water chestnuts, 2 chopped chives or shallots, 1 sprig of oregano (minced or ¼ teaspoon dried), 1 tablespoon soy sauce.

A tablespoon of homemade relish, ½ cup chopped mushrooms,sprig of marjoram (or ¼ teaspoon dried), salt and grind of pepper.

Garlic powder, sprig of rosemary and 1 tablespoon chopped parsley.

A cup of grated cheddar cheese, garlic powder, a little dry white wine.

Ham

HAM LOAF

This is a super ham loaf recipe and is given here because it is good served cold with horseradish.

> 2 pounds ground lean pork
> 1 pound ground cured ham
> 2 eggs
> 1 cup Rice Krispies
> 2 teaspoons Worcestershire sauce
> A little milk

Crush Rice Krispies and combine with the pork, ham and eggs. Mix well, stir in sauce and add a little milk if it is not moist enough. Shape into loaf and bake uncovered in shallow pan for 1½ to 2 hours in 350 degree oven.

Baste with the following: ½ cup water, ¼ cup vinegar, ¼ cup brown sugar, 1 teaspoon mustard and 1 teaspoon maple or rum flavoring.

Poultry

CHICKEN TARRAGON

3 pounds cut-up chicken (I prefer chicken breasts)
1 small thinly sliced onion
2 tablespoons Safflower oil
2 tablespoons flour
1 cup chicken stock (or broth)
1 small bay leaf
2 sprigs tarragon leaves
grind of black pepper
1 cup sour cream

Brown seasoned chicken and onion in heavy pan or electric skillet. Remove chicken and add flour to pan. Blend gradually with stock and return chicken to pan along with the bay leaf. Cover and simmer until chicken is tender. Then add the chopped tarragon and grind of pepper. Cook another 5 minutes. Stir in cream and cook only until it is hot.

SALMON LOAF

1 can boned salmon
1 beaten egg
¼ cup milk
1 teaspoon horseradish
4 slices grated American Cheese
1 cup bread crumbs
¼ cup margarine

Soften the bread crumbs in milk and mix together the ingredients. Spread in a greased baking pan and sprinkle with a few buttered bread crumbs.

RAY'S SHRIMP COCKTAIL SAUCE

My husband has a reputation for making super shrimp cocktails. In fact, all three of our children have called home for the recipe. The sauce is good on beef, too.

6 tablespoons tomato catsup
2 tablespoons horseradish
1/8 teaspoon Tabasco sauce
4 tablespoons lemon juice
¼ teaspoon celery salt

Pastry

NEVER FAIL PIE CRUST
Stir 1 egg into 1 cup sweet milk, add 2 teaspoons vinegar, 5 cups flour, 2 cups shortening and 1½ teaspoons salt.

RHUBARB PIE
Cut rhubarb into 1-inch pieces and measure out 2 cups. Add 1½ cups sugar, 2 heaping tablespoons flour, 1 egg slightly beaten, pinch of salt and 2 tablespoons butter. Pour into pie shell and cover with top crust. Bake at 450 degrees for 30 to 40 minutes.

RHUBARB PINEAPPLE PIE
1½ cups rhubarb cut into small pieces
1 cup drained crushed pineapple
1 tablespoon tapioca
1 egg
1 cup sugar
1 tablespoon butter

Combine ingredients and let stand while making pastry for 2 crust pie. Bake at 450 degrees, 30 to 40 minutes.

Cake

RHUBARB MALLOW CAKE

Spread 10½ ounces miniature marshmallows in greased flour pan. Cover with mixture of 5 cups rhubarb, diced, 1 cup white sugar and ½ cup brown sugar. Prepare 1 box yellow cake mix. Spread on top and bake at 350 degrees for 45 minutes. Use 9'' x 13'' pan.

ROSE GERANIUM CAKE

Use your favorite white cake recipe or a mix and add 1 teaspoon rose water flavoring. Place a single layer of rose geranium leaves in the bottom of a greased cake pan and cover with batter. Use a fluffy frosting and tint pink with food coloring. Candied rose petals and mint leaves make a nice decoration.

Cookies

HERB COOKIES

Cream 1½ cup shortening with 1 cup brown sugar and 1 cup white sugar. Add 2 eggs, 1 tablespoon vanilla, 3 tablespoons vinegar, 1 teaspoon soda, 1 teaspoon salt, 4½ cups flour and add one of the following: 1 teaspoon ground cardamom; 1 teaspoon anise seed; or, after rolling dough into balls, dip cookie into ½ cup toasted sesame seeds. Press with fork and bake at 350 degrees.

MINT ICE CREAM

Steep 1 cup chopped fresh mint in 1 pint hot milk and 1 pint hot cream for 20 minutes. Strain out mint. Beat 8 egg yolks and work in 1 cup white sugar. Pour over the minted milk and cream. Whip and cook almost to boiling. Chill, add green vegetable coloring and freeze, stirring in 2 teaspoons creme de menthe when half frozen.

HERB CANDIES

Horehound, peppermint, borage, lovage, sesame and angelica are all herbs that make good hard candies. Here is a basic recipe: Make a syrup from 1 quart water and 1½ pounds white sugar and 1½ pounds brown sugar. Boil to 240 degrees. Add 1 teaspoon butter and boil without stirring until the temperature reaches 312 degrees.

Remove from fire and add 1 teaspoon lemon juice. Pour into buttered pan and when cool block into squares. To get the herb flavor of your choice, boil 1 ounce of the dried herb in the quart of water, strain out the herb and continue with the syrup step.

MARIGOLD CUSTARD

We use ¼ cup of dried petals or ½ cup fresh pot marigold petals steeped in 1 cup of hot milk. Strain. Beat 3 eggs lightly, add 1 teaspoon vanilla, pinch of salt, 2 cups of unsweetened condensed milk and the hot milk. Put into loaf pan and place this pan in another pan filled with warm water. Bake at 325 degrees until knife inserted comes out clean. Sprinkle with more petals or with nutmeg.

Please, Promise Me A Rose Garden!

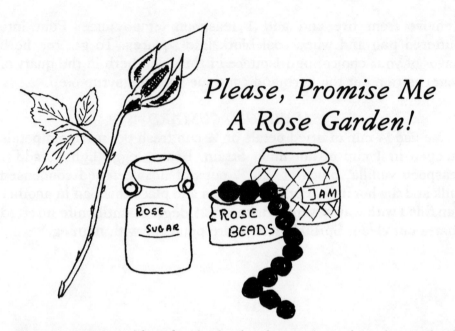

Roses aren't considered to be herbs, but can you imagine an herb garden without roses? Just the word "Rose" conjures up beauty, fragrance and romance.

King Charlemagne, who was with it when it came to herbs, said: "A rose is the friend of the cook and the praise of the physician." An apt description of an herb, wouldn't you agree?

In our own garden a lack of space prevents us from trying out the new modern roses. Because we are striving for fragrance and flavor we cultivate the very old roses. If you want to bring back the memorable fragrance of grandmother's garden, you can find these roses at "Tillotson's Roses." You will find their address in the back of this book. Their catalogue is a work of art and their stock, the finest.

Our rose garden features the following:

Rosa gallica officinalis—Apothecary Rose (before 1300). It has light crimson flowers which are intensely fragrant.

Rosa damascena bifera—ancient, the roses are pink and it blooms in autumn.

Salet—a moss rose, blooms repeatedly. A fragrant bloom from Salet is delightful as the center in a tussie mussie. (1854).

Crimson Glory is the only modern-day rose in my garden, but I love its big velvety, deep red petals for culinary purposes and potpourri.

Rosa damascena trigintipetala—(Prior to 1850). Blossoms are rose red. This is the rose grown in Bulgaria which is used for attar of roses—it takes 2,000 roses to produce one gram. No wonder it is worth its weight in gold. In fact, attar of roses is kept on deposit by the Bulgarian government in banks in Zurich, Paris and New York, and has steadily risen in price since World War II. It has rivaled the price of gold and platinum and in 1978 brought more than $3000 per kilo (2.2 pounds).

Most of the original cuttings in Bulgaria were brought from Persia during the 17th century to landscape the gardens of Turkish rulers. The rose found its way into the gardens of the common people and eventually became a commercial crop in the warm, sheltered valley (called the Valley of Roses) between the southern slopes of the Balkans and the northern foothills of the Sredna Gora.

During the last war, the Germans had the valley ploughed and sown with potatoes to prevent competition for a synthetic type of rose essence they were hoping to produce. Later it took five years to reintroduce the rose bushes. The roses are hand-plucked and harvested in May. The dew-filled crop must be picked between the hours of five and nine in the morning.

A receipt for "Ottar of Roses" in Mackenzie's *Five Thousand Receipts in all the Useful and Domestic Arts* (1831) is easy to follow.

"The Royal Society of Edinburgh received from Dr. Monro the following account of the manner in which this costly perfume is prepared in the east. Steep a large quantitiy of petals of the rose freed from every extraneous matter, in pure water, in an earthen or wooden vessel, which is exposed daily to the sun, and housed at night, till a scum rises to the surface. This is the ottar, which, carefully absorb by a very small piece of cotton tied to the end of a stick. The oil collected, squeeze out of the cotton into a very diminutive vial, stop it for use. The collection of it should be continued whilst any scum is produced.''

Another recipe is for Rose Perfume and is made with ''Hair Powder.'' A substitute would be 1 pound of cornstarch or rice powder. ''Strew a layer of rose leaves (fresh, dry damask roses), on sheets of paper, at the bottom of a box, cover them over with a layer of the powder, then strew alternately a layer of roses and a layer of powder. When they have lain 24 hours, sift the powder out and expose it to the air for 24 hours more. Stir it often. Add fresh rose leaves, twice, as before, and proceed in the same way; after this, dry the powder well in a gentle heat, and put it through a fine sieve. Lastly, pour 10 drops of rhodium, or 3 drops of ottor of roses in a fourth cup of sugar, triturate (grind) in a mortar, and stir well into the powder, which put into a box, or glass for use. This hair powder perfume will be excellent, and will keep well.''

ROSE WATER

Rose water is made by distillation, but we have a quick method for making it to use as a flavoring or for cosmetic purposes. It must be kept refrigerated.

Gather the rose petals in the morning, clip off the white tips, wash the petals, drain and pack loosely in a quart jar. Fill the jar with boiling water. Cap, shake the jar and let the contents steep overnight. The next day, drain off the petals and pour the rose water through a coffee filter. Bottle.

ROSE SYRUP NO. 1

Rose Syrup can be the base for some unusual desserts. Use 1 cup of rose water as prepared above to 2 cups of white sugar and 1 tablespoon fresh lemon juice. Stir and bring mixture to boiling point, making sure the sugar has dissolved. Pour into sterile jars and seal. This can be used on pancakes, crepes with a filling of raspberries, on ice cream sundaes, in punch and cake frosting.

ROSE SYRUP NO. 2

Wash 2 quarts of rose petals, clip off white heels and spread out on screen to dry for several days. Put into kettle and barely cover with water, add 3 cups of white sugar and 1 tablespoon lemon juice. Boil gently until the mixture begins to thicken (takes about 5 to 10 minutes). Then strain through a coffee filter, bottle and seal tightly. It will improve as it ages.

ROSE HONEY

Put a layer of partially dried rose petals in the electric skillet and cover with a thin, mild honey. Keep the temperature very low and let it heat enough to shrink the petals. Strain and bottle. Other honey flavors may be made in the same manner. The honey is better if it ages for a few weeks.

A Conserve of Flowers was used as a medication, "a comforter of the hart and spirits, and to expel any malignant or pestilential quality gathered neere thereon." The recipes are quite simple.

ROSE CONSERVE

Take freshly picked and washed rose petals, place whole in a crock, cover with very fine sugar and set in sun for several days. Keep a thin layer of cheesecloth tied over the mixture to keep out insects. One tablespoon of the conserve will take care of much "comforting and expelling."

Let's face it; everyone is not going to "dig" rose flavoring, but, I believe it is just the idea of eating flowers. They haven't been conditioned. A sneaky way to find out if they like the flavor is to use a little rose sugar on desserts. Don't tell them what it is and if their opinion isn't "candied,"—forget it!

ROSE SUGAR

Pick a perfect, fragrant rose bud (one that has not been sprayed with an insecticide). Place in a pint jar filled with white sugar and set it in the sun. Leave it there for 2 weeks. The sugar will be ready.

This same method will work for other flowers, seeds and herbs. A vanilla bean kept in a jar of white sugar is also nice to keep on hand.

ROSE JAM

This is a variation of rose syrup No. II. Cook the mixture until it flakes from the spoon. Pack in sterile jars and seal. Baby food jars are a nice size for this, but they require a thin layer of paraffin.

ROSE PETAL PARFAIT

1 small box gelatin (red raspberry or strawberry)
2 cups minus 2 tablespoons boiling water
2 tablespoons of rose water (added to above)

Prepare gelatin in the usual way and let partly congeal. Put a layer of gelatin then a layer of whipped cream (this could be sweetened with a little rose-flavored sugar) and another layer of gelatin and cream into parfait glasses. Layers of drained red raspberries or strawberries make an even prettier and more flavorful parfait. Top with whipped cream and a candied rosebud.

ROSE HIP SAUCE
(From *The Housekeeper's Encyclopedia,* 1861)

This sauce is to be poured over cottage pudding. Open and remove seed from rose hips. Soak them and boil until tender, reducing the hips to a paste. Pass them through a sieve, stir them in boiling wine and sweeten to taste. The sauce should be as thick as thin cream.

EXTRACT OF ROSE

Take a gallon bottle, fill it nearly full of rose leaves (petals) packed tight, and fill the bottle with the best brandy; as the leaves dissolve, add more.

CANDIED ROSE PETALS

This recipe works for rose petals, violets, lilac blossoms and herb leaves. First, we have an easy method—whip an egg white (lightly) then take a clean watercolor brush and very lightly brush the petals with the egg white. Sift fine sugar over them and put aside to dry thoroughly before storing them between layers of waxed paper in a tin box. If you place the petals on a wire or mesh screen which is elevated a few inches, the drying process may be speeded up.

We will skip the plain old syrup method, I have tried it and my violets came out looking like flies.

You will have good success if you take this preliminary precaution. Dissolve an ounce of gum arabic (available at the drug store) in ½ cup of water (over a double boiler) and let it cool. Using a clean pair of tweezers, dip each petal, leaf or blossom into the heavy liquid, hold it up a second to drain and then put it on the screen to dry. The gum arabic gives the flowers a leathery surface and makes the syrup adhere better.

Now to make the syrup. Boil 1 cup of white sugar with ½ cup water and 1 tablespoon corn syrup. Bring up to 238 degrees on the candy thermometer and let the syrup cool. Dip the blossoms in carefully, drain quickly and sift granulated sugar over them, covering both the top and undersides. When perfectly dry, pack as directed in other method. For more attractive results, tint the syrup and the sugar to match the blossom. You can buy colored sugar in almost any shade today.

ROSE BUTTER

Put half-layer of unsalted butter into a crock or jar. Add a layer of washed, fresh rose petals and continue layering until the jar is almost full. Store in the refrigerator for 4 or 5 days before using. As you use the butter, discard the layers of petals.

ROSE PETAL SANDWICHES

Cut bread into rounds, spread with the rose butter and place red or pink petals on top.

So, smell your flowers and eat them too!

AND MORE ROSES

"You may break, you may ruin, the vase if you will,
But the scent of the Roses will hang round it still."

We covered potpourri and sachets in an earlier chapter, but there is another rose item that is really nostalgic and could become popular again today. I remember when I was a child my mother would let me go through her jewelry drawer. Tucked away in their own box was a string of beads made from rose petals. She had them for many years, but when one removed the lid the fragrance of rose was still there. Needless to say, after you picked them up the fragrance was transferred to your hands.

My girl friends and I would try to make the beads, but only made some messes. Years later, an old friend told me how she had made them when she was a girl. When I followed her directions, the rose beads "came out right."

Gather petals in the morning as soon as the dew evaporates. Use the most fragrant roses. Put them through a food grinder, using the finest blade. Now add a teaspoon of salt per quart of petals and put through the food chopper again. You should have a mass which is smooth textured. Put this into an iron skillet and barely cover with water (use any juice that came out when grinding) and heat thoroughly; do not, however, let the mixture boil. Reheat and stir the mixture once a day for 3 days. by now it should be black and pulpy. Rub some safflower or olive oil on your hands and pat the mixture into a layer about 1/8 inch thick on waxed paper. Roll to make it even. Cut out the beads with a thimble, roll in your hands and push a hole through the center of each bead with a thin wire. Sometimes I put a long, thin needle into a cork and just push the beads one at a time into the needle. Let dry.

Before stringing them, I soak the beads overnight in a mixture of safflower oil to which I have added a few drops of rose oil. Polish with a soft cloth and string. If you want a matte finish, do not polish.

Sources For Herbs, Seeds, Plants And Products

Well-Sweep Herb Farm
317 Mt. Bethel Road
Port Murray, New Jersey 07865
     Catalog is 35 cents

Yankee Peddler Herb Farm
Dept. D Highway 36 N
Brenham, Texas 77833
     Catalog is $1.00, refundable with order

Sunnybrook Farms Nursery
9448 Mayfield Road
Chesterland, Ohio 44026
     Catalog is 50 cents, refundable with order

Roses of Yesterday and Today
(formerly Tillotson's)
802 Brown's Valley Road
Watsonville, California 95076
     Catalog is $1.00 and is published
     once annually in the fall.

Caswell-Massey Pharmacy
518 Lexington Avenue (Corner of 48th St.)
New York, New York 10017